SKIMMING THE CREAM

SKIMMING THE CREAM

Fifty Years With Peggy of the Flint Hills

by

Zula Bennington Greene

Baranski Publishing Company

FIRST EDITION

Copyright © 1983 by Zula Bennington Greene

All Rights Reserved under International and
Pan-American Copyright Conventions

Published in the United States of America
by the Baranski Publishing Company, Topeka, Kansas

ISBN 0-941974-04-9

Jacket Design by
Vic Eisenhut-Graphic Arts, Inc., Topeka, Kansas

Cover Photograph by
Carol Neff-Barton Photography, Topeka, Kansas

Editorial Assistance by Theresa Slover

Photo Credits:
Topeka Capital-Journal
Jayhawker Studio
J.W. Hill Studio
Washburn University
Topeka Civic Theatre
Olan Mills

PRINTED IN THE UNITED STATES OF AMERICA

Preface

It doesn't seem like fifty years. My feelings are like Jacob's. You know he worked seven years for Rachel, got the wrong girl, then worked seven more years and it seemed unto him but a few days, for the love he had for her.

In 1933 my husband and I, with our two young children, moved from the Flint Hills of Kansas to Topeka. I had been writing a column for several weekly newspapers and in Topeka I began writing a column, six days a week, for the Daily Capital, now the Capital-Journal.

Unlike most columns, mine is not about a single subject, but about any topic I might fancy. It may be about the sunrise, about the baby's new tooth, politics, the changing seasons, my cat, or about hanging out clothes on a sunny day under a bluing blue sky.

I began writing for the Capital the year that President Franklin Roosevelt first took office and, casting a backward look, it does seem a long time. These fifty years have witnessed the coming of television, a man on the moon, doors that open even without saying "Sesame," nylon stockings, electronics, down-filled jackets and wash and wear clothing.

Fifty years, six days a week, adds up to about 15,000 columns. Skimming the cream for this book was done with the help of friends. They came and we read through fifty years, comparing, choosing, and after three skimmings, the selections were made, but not without some pain. Members of the Topeka Civic Theatre were involved from the beginning, particularly Jim Robertson and Marlyn Burch, and throughout the printing.

Theresa Slover organized the reading and selection and prepared the manuscript for printing, which is not mentioning the heavy books she lugged to the copier or the records she kept. Beth Sheffel, Mabel Remmers and Jean Saylor read and chose, as did my daughter, Dorothy Hanger, who assisted greatly in many other ways. I appreciate the special work of Virginia Eicholtz and W. Robert Alderson, Jr. And my warm thanks to John H. Stauffer, publisher of the Capital-Journal, for his help and encouragement, and to all my friends "at the paper" for their support.

Putting this book together with the help of kind and generous friends was a rich experience that will be remembered.

Topeka, Kansas
October 19, 1983

Zula Bennington Greene

Introduction

For fifty years, "Peggy of the Flint Hills," has graced the pages of the Topeka Capital-Journal. I remember growing up and looking for Zula Bennington Greene's column just as one looked for a favorite columnist, cartoon or sports writer. The secret of her enduring charm, I believe, is her thoughtfulness, interest and concern in all things great and small.

In the tumult and shouting of events which push us this way and that, "Peggy of the Flint Hills," never seemed pessimistic. A sense of civility and common sense gave the reader a shared feeling of comfort. All is right with the world when one can view it from the perspective of the Kansas Flint Hills. Trials and tribulations there will be, but thanks to "Peggy" we know there is beauty in our land and goodness in our neighbors—Thank you, "Peggy of the Flint Hills" for caring and sharing.

—Senator Nancy Landon Kassebaum

*With thoughts of Willard
and for all of ours.*

Table of Contents

Preface . . . . *iii*

Introduction . . . . *v*

I. 1933 - 1940 1

II. 1941 - 1949 31

    Photographs 89

III. 1950 - 1959 99

IV. 1960 - 1969 127

    Photographs 149

V. 1970 - 1983 157

I
1933-1940

Foreword—Strictly Personal

We were the second child and second daughter in our family. It has always been our theory, though the subject has been too painful ever to discuss with our parents, that they desired a boy for their second child and were so confident of the fulfillment of their wish, that they had considered no feminine names at all, and were utterly unprepared to bestow a suitable name on a girl baby. They had been let down and they were hurt and disappointed.

We have never believed that there was any talk of drowning us, but our anguished parents turned us over, to be named, to a grandmother who had lived and suffered, having had 10 children, and a maiden aunt who had lived and made others suffer. These two estimable female relatives gave us the name of Zula Christina, the latter being the grandmother's own name and the former a name the romantic maiden aunt had picked up in some of the books she read.

With this foreword, gentle reader, it is easy to understand why we acquired the name of "Peggy." When our first effort at a column appeared in the Chase County Leader five years ago and W. C. Austin, the editor, now state printer, hoping to call a little attention to it, labeled it "By Peggy" we bearing the un-Christian name of Zula Christina, were certainly not one to protest, and thankfully accepted it.

And that, my dears, is the answer often asked us, "How did you happen to choose the name of Peggy?" We didn't choose it. It was thrust upon us.
—December 11, 1933

1

In Re Jury Duty

Out of the travail of stark necessity comes the dawn of a new idea. There is no need to lament that many were called but few were chosen for the Finney jury. Rather, one should throb with pride for the high degree of literacy in our dear beloved Kansas.

But in the future juries need not be selected. Jurors will be born, not made. In the medieval baronies, the hangmen were a class apart, distinctive, honored in a way, feared, shunned. The business was hereditary. The oldest son took his father's place and the other sons must find hangmen jobs, that is, as many as could be absorbed under the code. The daughters must marry sons of hangmen and become mothers of hangmen. They were a sort of nobility in themselves.

It would be our idea that we should breed a class of jurors in this country. Children would be dedicated to jury service by noble, sacrificing parents and, like the Spartan children, taken from their mothers when they were seven weeks old. Theirs would be a sacred service rendered to the state.

High walls would surround them all their lives and not a single scrap of written or printed matter would be allowed within the gates. There would be no schools, no reading, no history or poetry, for their minds must be absolutely unbiased.

Mother Goose rhymes and bedtime stories would be strictly forbidden lest they form opinions about Tom, Tom, the piper's son, who stole a pig, or about the wicked step-sisters of Cinderella. Opinions are not for jurors.

These jurors would be on tap at all times and all a judge would need to do would be to phone and say send me twelve jurors and there they would be by return mail. No questions, no fuss, no waiting, and a jury unbiased, unprejudiced, who had not read the papers, discussed the case or formed an opinion. The evidence would fall upon the virginal minds of twelve noble souls dedicated to the sacred service of the state.

Then, indeed, would justice shine forth as the morning star and proudly cast away the bandage from her eyes.

—December 21, 1933

*   *   *

During that bad dust storm, someone made the remark that when it did rain, it would rain mud, and that is just what it did. Even the Saturday night rain did not entirely clear the air of dust, for the Sunday sprinkle rained mud on a car which had been washed up shiny and clean.

—May 15, 1934

What-a-Man Finney

And so the prison gates have shut behind Ronald Finney, now known as No. 4224, and it may be for years and it may be forever, according to the sentence imposed by Judge Heinz.

"None of us have ever seen a man like him!" passionately declared a

2

defense attorney during the recent impeachment cases, speaking of Ronald Finney. The plea of the accused state officials was that Finney fooled them all. He impressed everybody.

He had the proper social and financial background, powerful friends, a magnetic personality, charming manners. In fact, he had everything. They all trusted him like a brother, from the clerks of the little red schoolhouse to the big fellows from Chicago and Washington.

Certain it is that Finney has shown himself a sporting prisoner. He has not winced nor cried aloud. Instead of being stubbornly rebellious during his local incarceration, he nobly gave himself to improving the game of contract played by his associates, many of whom, poor fellows, did not have the advantages which he had had of being raised in a good Christian home.

Finney has the spirit of daring and the ability to take it. With these qualities, had he had a normal moral and ethical sense, the name of Ronald Finney might have been almost as well known as it is now, but in a more honorable line of endeavor.

The question is, should we be taking notes for the literature of the future? Will a hundred years clothe Ronald Finney with the romantic glamour which time has given Francois Villon, Robin Hood, Captain Kidd and Jesse James?

For it is not the purely good whose memory is kept green by the world, but the dashing, the romantic, the imaginative. Judas is as well remembered as John, and Cleopatra as Cecelia.

—June 4, 1934

The Heat Dragon

Tuesday night the heat dragon came and breathed his hot breath over the earth.

The human race has developed courage. Daily men brave danger and risk death and women stand immobile through pain and disaster and defeat.

But there is one thing against which we are helpless—the fear of the unknown. It is a heritage from savagery when falling stars and shooting comets were the acts of gods and left man stricken and helpless.

We are still stricken and helpless against the devastations of nature. The heat dragon is displeased with us and for many days he has tortured us with his hot breath, burning our crops and threatening our animals with starvation. We have offended him and he is drying up the earth.

All day he snorts in anger and lashes his tail, but at night he goes back to his home in the sun and lies down to sleep. Then for a few brief hours the earth becomes cool and man can rest.

But Tuesday he came back in the night. The stars and trees were still, trembling with sighs of weariness and preparing themselves for their rest.

Then suddenly his hot breath was over the earth, mysterious and strange, searing and suffocating.

Why had he come back? Within the memory of man, his hot breath had not been felt at night. There was an undercurrent of danger, a stir, the restlessness of impending doom. So must Siegfried have felt when he first learned the meaning of fear.

People looked into each other's faces for the comfort they knew would not be there and waited in silent agony for the dawn. It came at last and the flaming monster, spent with his night of fury, crept back to the sun for a little rest.

The weather bureau bravely said things the next morning about low pressure and barometric readings, but it didn't fool anybody. The people knew that the wrath of the heat dragon had been visited upon the earth.

—August 3, 1934

Star Dust

Several times we saw them, as unaware of the crowds about them as if they had been the first couple, and the roaring, whirling, bawling, milling, glittering mass which makes up a fair had been the quiet, tangled haunts of a primitive Eden.

They were unmistakably from the country. Her eyes were soft and big and brown, the frank, trusting eyes of one who has never been given cause for doubting the world about her. His were bright blue sparks between narrowed lids, the habitual protection of a man who spends his life in the sun and wind, and his tanned face was several shades darker than his blond hair.

They walked about in a kind of a stunned way their arms linked together and their hands clasped, bewilderment on their faces and star dust in their eyes.

The jerky amusement rides furnished ample excuse for his arm to encircle her soft, yielding body in its simple red dress, and for her blowing brown hair, only slightly covered by a small red hat, to seek the lodestone of his shoulder.

After that they drank some pop, tho perhaps they could not have told you what it was, for they were drinking, not soda water, but the wonder of each other.

Later we observed them in the grandstand, sitting close to each other on a high seat. When the horses were on the last exciting home stretch and the crowd serged to its feet, they drew instinctively together and the boy hurriedly slipped his arm for a breathless instant about her waist.

He looked at her instead of at the horses, at her deep, dark eyes, her full red mouth, her smooth throat. And she looked at him. For what woman would not give her soul to be looked at as he looked at her? The streak of quivering horseflesh on the track was not so thrillingly alive as the fire trembling within themselves.

They were in love.

4

Perhaps they will be coming back to the fair next year, but the honeymoon will be about over by then. They will not hold hands or strive for a swift, electric touch of each other. They may take a bottle of pop, but they will not ride on the bumpy joy-rides, and they will look at the horses instead of each other.

The next year the girl will have to stay at home with the baby, but in another year she can lead him around by the hand. She may wear the same red dress, made over according to the current styles, but surely she will have a new hat.

In a dozen years the young man, not so young any more, will divide his time between the hogs he brought in to the fair and the trapeze performers. The girl in the red dress will be wearing serviceable navy blue and spending her time in the canning department, and trying to keep her young from sudden and violent destruction.

She will stand by and watch them ride on the merry-go-round, and if anybody should happen to notice her, which is quite unlikely, as she has put on weight and lost her slim, young softness, she would be just another mother waiting for the ride to end.

But perhaps she will be thinking of another fair, when she rode with madness in her heart, when burning eyes flashed deathless messages quicker then Marconi ever dreamed of.

And perhaps she will be wondering, with a panicky, cold fear tearing at her heart, if she is never to know madness again, never to feel again the wild thrill of love, if life will continue to stretch out, wider and wider before her, and never give her one more flaming, glistening hour to hold against the midnight blue of other days.

They will sit in the grandstand again, but the star dust will be gone from their eyes and there will be only the dust from the race track. They will be less aware of each other than of the post which obstructs their view of the running horses. The fire in their eyes will be drained into rivulets of new life.

Soon they will look back and begin to wonder why they do not have fairs like they used to, for instance, like that one they had in 1934. That was a fair! Such horses! Such pop! Such weather! And such a moon hanging in the western sky by a single silvery tip!

But there will never be such a fair again. Nor such horses. Nor such a moon. For a fair like that can be seen only thru a prism of star dust. And you have to be young and in love to have star dust in your eyes.

—September 18, 1934

Child Warriors

Our little boy is nine years old. In regard to the harsher things of life, he is still a baby. He and his friends play at war and robber with no idea whatever of the cruel reality back of them. Yet if he lived in Italy, he would, by the latest mandate of Mussolini, be entering a career of military service.

Mussolini began his lordship over Italy as a "benevolent dictator," taking charge of Italy in the chaotic conditions following the years of the war. There is little doubt but that he has unified and stabilized that country.

But the price to the Italian people has been too high. He has removed women from industrial jobs only recently so that they may bear more children. And what for? His latest order answers that question, an order that little boys of eight and over must be given military training.

When any people surrender their common rights as citizens and as human beings, they are putting their heads into nooses of political slavery. A dictator, no matter how benevolent, if given enough power, will become a despot. A nation or an individual must manage their own affairs, no matter how badly, or close the door upon liberty.

The last monstrous move of the dictator of Italy to teach little children the beginning of hate, to prepare them to kill, will be either the final death knell of that nation or the beginning of freedom. Sometimes, in order for things to get better, they must get pretty bad. A disease must run its course and pass the crisis before recovery can begin. A nation, like people, will often stand for a good deal before asserting themselves to the point of rebellion.

Surely the parents of Italy, if they have love for their children and love of freedom in their hearts, will revolt before the spectacle of war being taught to babies. If they do not, then there is no spark of liberty in them and the soil of Italy will witness the greatest tyranny of her stormy, bloody years.

—September 29, 1934

Winter Dusk

It has been a long time, as the crow flies, since I have been on a train, so it was in a spirit of adventure that I took a Santa Fe to Wichita Sunday afternoon.

Driving one's own car or hopping a bus is convenient, but when roads are slick and storms swirl thru the air, the good old steam horse gives one a sense of security.

I found that parting scenes had not changed. The same men were there with the same swift dutiful kisses for the same women, or very similar ones. Men are like that. They are pretty sure to stick to the same type of woman, tho they change the model occasionally. People still said, "Well, take care of yourself," and they still shivered outside, waiting for the last wave thru the window as the train pulled out.

The first time I ever rode on a train was when I was six years old and we went to visit Uncle John's and Uncle Ike's folks in Oklahomy, Uncle Ike being a preacher and the father of 12 children.

We packed enough fried chicken and cake and pie and baked ham and pickles to last us—my father, mother, three children, an uncle and aunt—the entire trip, and I can vividly recall the thrill of opening the telescope and partaking of these dainties when it was time for a meal.

But now not even the shelled pecans and bananas could make me hungry.

My brother and I spent much time composing words to suit the rhythm of the wheels beating against the tracks. He said it sounded like "where the bloom makes a whistle in the wallow" and I declared it was "thundery, dundery, undery."

The tall young man across the aisle, in the gray suit and gray spats has just put down his crossword puzzle and is reading "The men in Garbo's glamorous life."

A winter landscape is a symbol of waiting. The trees stand motionless, bracing themselves against the ground with windmill etched blackly against the gray sky. A farmer going home with a load of wood, the horses fuzzy and ungraceful in their winter coats. A creek, slate-gray under a gray sky.

The sun retires early, hastily, apologetic that its efforts for the day have been so futile. Even the glow which it leaves is pale lemon-colored, without a look of warmth, which quickly fades to a yellow-gray, across which the trees move, like black-robed figures in a tragedy, as stark and hard and uncompromising as truth.

The twinkling lights of a town. A brakeman's lantern appearing and disappearing at each swift stride. And across the thin landscape the sound of a whistle, lonely and forlorn and sad.

The young man across the aisle has made himself a comfortable bed with two seats and an extra cushion and is doubtless dreaming of Garbo or a three-letter word meaning an Australian beast of burden.

We arrived and found the Peerless Princess of the Plains in what the town's largest paper referred to as "the throes of a gripping blizzard." My hostess, Mrs. Ray Foley, had sent her husband and nephew to meet me and with no more event than a live wire falling across our path, we ended the journey.

I was put on the davenport before a fire and Mr. Foley fetched a blanket to throw over me while Mrs. Foley ran to get the cough syrup. I haven't had so much babying since I went to visit my parents and came down with mumps, and it was too bad that I began to get better right away.

—January 23, 1935

* * *

The government will not need to retire that submarginal land out in western Kansas. It has blown away. . . . It is said that a friend of Frank Carlson got a letter from him saying he was pretty homesick since he smelled some of the dirt from his farm as it passed over Washington.

A Garden City housewife can't decide whether to clean the back porch or plant the garden there.

—March 29, 1935

Rain

Dripping softly comes the rain
Like the still white peace
That follows pain.
Or like a torrent of blinding tears,
Bitter repentance
For wasted years.
Nature teaching once again.
He knows no joy
Who has felt no pain.

It rained and the world is clean and new. Not only dust, but despair was washed away. There has been no such wave of happiness since the signing of the armistice. Even those indirectly affected beam like the bride's father at a wedding.

Something has happened. It's historic. A revival sweeping the town couldn't have done it, nor a successful political campaign. Everybody's happy and it's no matter at all now about the NRA, the AAA or the CCC. They can do what they please in Washington. Out here in Kansas we've started to farm and we've got no time for political foolishness.

But this feeling of joy. It's like a soldier coming home to a clean soft bed after the mud and vermin of trenches, like having sugar in your coffee again, like falling in love when you're fifty. It's getting back something you haven't had for a long time that you can't live without.

—May 17, 1935

*   *   *

A young woman who has a position teaching music in a small town for the coming year is going to need the wisdom of Solomon, the patience of Job, and the tact of a diplomat to get along.

The president of the school board has written her that both he and the secretary of the board belong to the Methodist church and they would like to have her worship there every Sunday and use her talents for the glory of God and the followers of John Wesley.

The other member of the school board wrote that both her daughters expect to take private lessons from the new teacher and that they would like to have her take charge of the Presbyterian music during the school year. The Presbyterian church, she adds, is really the nicest church in town. Their preacher wears a frock coat and black tie every Sunday, while every other preacher in town just preaches in an ordinary suit.

—May 31, 1935

In the Cemetery

It's a little too late for peonies—
Just see how these white ones shatter
When I lift them out.
I guess it doesn't matter,
They wouldn't last long, anyway

8

Yes, mother lived to be eighty-three
And didn't look a day
Over sixty. Did you know Marie
Is here?
I've never seen the roses
Nicer than they are this year.

Nell's over there putting flowers
On the graves of her two children.
They say she spends hours
Out here.
I don't think it pays to keep on grieving
After a person is gone—
Of course she lives near
And doesn't mind leaving
Her work. She was always kind of queer.
One day when I happened to pass
By, I saw them spreading
A lunch down on the grass.
Well, I may be kind of odd,
But I think a graveyard's a funny place
To have a picnic. Did that man nod
To us?

There's poor Lillian
Just sitting there with her hands around her knees.
Grace thinks she is losing her mind.
She never sees
Anyone around her. And once when a man came to find
His mother's grave and asked her
Who was buried by that tall
Monument, she said, "I am." It's strange
She never married again,
For after all,
The world is full of good men.
Shall we speak
To Mary? Yes, he took pneumonia
And didn't last a week.
Those iris have spread
Till they don't amount to much.
All the Herricks are dead
But the old man. I never saw such
A grand day. There he is
Putting wild flowers on Lucy's grave
And looking at his
Own name on the monument and the place they save
For him, thinking, maybe,
That by next year he'll be there beside her.

That silly Mrs. Snyder
Said she'd put flowers on him when he was dead.
"Thank you, ma'am," he said,
"I won't need no flowers. I'll have Lucy."

Hold this vase a minute.
While I get some water to put in it.
That's a fine stone they put up for Esther—
It must have cost a plenty.
I was there when they carried her in dead,
She was only twenty.
Don't you remember how pretty she looked in her coffin?
Like a bride, people said.
(She hadn't wasted away by sickness).

Look at the thickness
Of this last
Bed of portulaca.
Poor Mr. Kent is bringing flowers
For his boy who shot himself.
I never saw anybody break so fast.
H'm, Flossie and Flonnie are funny names for twins. Died two hours
        after they were born
March 25, 1884—
The letters are getting worn,
See if you can make out any more.

Could you hand me that bucket lid?
My, this pump works hard.
I don't think Ward
Takes care of the cemetery like Henry did.
He used to mow grass by the hour.
His grave hasn't sunk much yet,
Has it? I forget—
What is it they call this blue flower?

—June 1, 1935

*   *   *

There is something I must speak of. Having just been to Washington, I would not be doing my duty if I did not remind Mrs. Landon that the White House is an old done-over building, even more ancient than the governor's residence in Topeka. There are dozens of fireplaces, a piano done in 15 colors and gold which must be a fright to keep looking decent, and huge mirrors which will be terrible to get fly-specked in summer.

The rooms are full of portraits of solemn men with beards and women in odd-looking clothes. People tramp through the house all day and there is company for nearly every meal. Her husband's office will be right in the house and any woman knows how hard it is to get her work done with a man under foot all day.

But if, knowing these things, she wants to encourage her husband in any ambitions he may have to be president, I'm for him.

—August 27, 1935

Winter

The first cold spell is always the hardest. Shivering as I dressed a few mornings ago I thought how nice it would be if I could pack up the family and depart for southern waters along about the first of November every year. Being cold makes one so miserable.

And since there is no harm in wishing, I thought it would be nice to stay away until the first of April and trip north again with the spring.

By that time I decided, being dressed and feeling more cheerful, that I wouldn't mind staying in Kansas until after Thanksgiving. I like to see that creeping up of winter, the fall of the last leaves, the bleak landscape huddling patiently close to the earth.

There is something about the still cold twilight of a November day that I would miss in Florida, the thin bare sound of whistles, hurrying figures with heads shrunk into collars, a silence in the air, a sadness, a forlornness, but not a hopelessness, rather an acceptance as quiet as a thin blue spiral of smoke.

And having stayed past Thanksgiving, with Christmas decorations going up, I would probably decide not to leave until the first of the year. It is fun to walk with someone you like very much, jostling about in the crowds of shoppers, and see the bright windows thru a soft snow. Christmas might not be the same in a bathing suit. We'd just stay past New Year and then take a little trip.

I know what would happen then. Spring would be near, if not in fact, then in the flood of seed catalogs, spring style books, and new straw hats. January will soon pass, February is a short month, and then March will be here, with robins and pussy willows and swelling buds.

I wouldn't want to miss the first pale yellow-green leaves coming out in lacy delicacy, and sometimes spring comes early. It would hardly be safe to wait until the first of April to see it bursting in Kansas.

The year would not be complete without the silence of a winter day in the country, when the earth is hushed and sleeping, when trees stand straight and black against a gray sky, when furry cattle huddle on the south side of a straw stack, and the only sound is a wagon creaking with feed, the breaths of the man and horses making a fog in the cold air.

But suppose I should go away and come back for the spring? Returning from the exotic profusion of palms and magnolias, would I be thrilled with a slender pale green leaf on a black stem? Spring is release, freedom from the bondage of winter, joy over returning warmth and life.

But suppose there was no winter. How could anyone love the spring

11

who had not known the winter? What thrill would there be in running streams if you had not seen them icebound? What gratitude could there be for warmth if you had not been cold?

There can not be day without night, joy without sorrow, nor spring without winter.

Author's note: All readers who do not expect to go South this winter file the above away for the cold comfort it may bring when sharp winds blow and snow flies in the air. Personally, I expect the comfort to be so cold that I shall not bother with it.

—November 7, 1935

Equal Rights

The National Woman's party proposes an amendment to the constitution giving women equal rights with men. A good many men may wonder what in heaven's name they have now if it isn't equal rights, but there are a thousand state laws, a leader says, which deprive women of the "right to earn a livelihood."

I would not be surprised if the movement was started by a lady who desires to be either the governor of Oklahoma or an elder in the Presbyterian church, two positions to which I believe women can not now aspire.

A good many women, incidentally, still blame Saint Paul for their lowly position, and I'll admit he did speak out of turn several times. I have often thought that one of the first things I am going to do, when I am settled in my mansion in the skies and have had my mail changed to the new address, got used to the feel of wings and practiced on the harp a little—one of the first things I am going to do is hunt up Saint Paul and start an argument with him. The chances are that Susan B. Anthony and other good ladies who have passed on have already spoken to him and he ought not be hard to handle.

I desire to state that I am in favor of anything which will advance the cause of women, and that I will address letters, hand out bills, speak on street corners, march in parades, or go to jail if I can help my sisters to secure whatever they want to secure.

But I believe they are tackling the problem from the wrong end. I think they could get the amendment into the constitution all right, for politicians are always skittish of the woman vote and would feel that it was a harmless way to quiet them, but having equal rights on the pages of the constitution would be merely scaling the foothills.

The ladies would do well to remember, as the wets and drys have found out, that constitutions, like treaties, are scraps of paper unless they are also written on the hearts of the people. Government is the will of the majority and you can no more make an unpopular sentiment liked by placing it on

12

the law books than you can make a man love a woman at the point of a shotgun.

The Versailles treaty is falling to pieces because the provisions never did represent the desires of all the signers. You can push people and force them, by one means or another, to do things which they do not want to do, but some day the tide will come rolling back and they will rebel.

One of the leaders complains that men never pass laws to keep women from working 24 hours a day in the home and that it is only when their own jobs are threatened that they pass laws to protect ladies from overwork.

The lady is dead right, but she will have to admit that as a class women employes are not as stable as men. An employer never knows, when he hires a woman, how soon she may be married and leave or when her work may be interrupted by child-bearing. A man who marries and becomes a father can be counted on to stick a little closer to his post than ever.

If the woman should get equal rights, I wonder if they would also want equal responsibility. Would they advocate the repeal of laws which place financial and moral responsibility on men? Would they seek to remove laws requiring men to pay alimony or agree themselves to be liable for the support of a former husband?

Men and women can never be identical, and I see no use in beating my brains out against a stone wall because of it.

And that is why I believe the ladies are working on the wrong end of the problem. What they should do is get an amendment to the constitution changing certain biological customs which have been in vogue for some time.

In my opinion the time is ripe for a change, the iron is hot. Here is the New Deal with a bunch of moneys—I used to not know when to use the word "moneys," but my rule now is that anything over a billion is "moneys." Under that amount, the singular is used. What better use could the administration make of these large sums than to further a biological reform of a system which everybody admits is a distinct disadvantage to women?

Women's struggles to achieve economic equality come right back to their old enemy, biology, and no matter what they can get written on the statutes, they can't do much to change conditions—unless some of our best braintrusters can perform a miracle.

—December 5, 1935

*   *   *

An old woman who had never had much was seeing the ocean for the first time. She sat down and folded her hands and looked at it. "It's the first thing I've ever seen that there's enough of," she sighed—.

—December 31, 1935

13

A Baby Speaks

It makes me laugh when I think how simple I used to be. Only a few months ago I thought that all I needed to make me happy was to learn to walk. Then I couldn't be plumped down while the rest of the family frisked off into another room. Also I could get to some of the pretty things around the house.

It just shows how little I knew about life. In the first place, walking was not as easy as it looked to be. I thought I would be able to skip through the house like my brother, but I found out that it was real hard work. A person sometimes sat down suddenly or fell forward and mashed his nose. Of course I don't fall down much any more and I am getting used to bumps.

One day I saw some pretty cloth hanging off the table. When I pulled on it I sat right down on the floor and it came along with me. It was nice and soft. I wound it around my hands and rubbed it over my face. I was having fun.

Then my mother came into the room. She grabbed the pretty cloth and said, "My new dress!" in a way that made me feel sad. She set me down hard on a chair and I was awful still for a while. Then something came swelling up in my throat and the tears poured out of my eyes.

After I had cried a while I got down and walked around. I saw something shiny on the table and I reached up and got it. It would open and shut and make a nice clicking noise. I was happy again and walked out to show my mother the nice thing I had found.

But I saw something was wrong and I shut my eyes, thinking I would be set down hard again. But I wasn't. My mother picked me up and said, "Dotty darling! The scissors! My precious baby." Her voice didn't make me sad this time and my throat didn't start swelling inside.

She carried me to a chair and held me close against her, warm and nice. She rocked me and sang a little song that made me feel sleepy.

I'm learning a lot about life. It is mostly divided into two parts. Some things you get kissed for and some things you get set down hard for. It's all in knowing which is which.

—March 18, 1936

The Flint Hills

Marco Morrow has asked me to settle an argument between two old timers and tell him just where are the Flint Hills.

Flint Hills is the name given by the early settlers to those rolling, normally green-covered pastures in Kansas beginning in northern Greenwood county, extending into southern Morris county, and embracing all counties lying between. The term is somewhat loosely applied to a much larger area, from Cowley and Chautauqua counties in the north and from Coffey to Marion counties across the beam, but this is merely a pre-election use of the term and should not be taken too seriously.

Ask anyone who lives there and he will tell you that the Flint Hills are the best grazing lands on earth. In some miraculous manner, with the addition of nothing but salt and water, they put fat on cattle and finish them for market.

Residents of Greenwood county claim that Eureka is the heart of the Flint Hills, but Chase county farmers who live around Bazaar, while they may humor the Greenwood county folks, know better. Before the railroad was extended to Matfield Green about 10 years ago, the little village of Bazaar was the largest shipping point of cattle in the state. Every spring hundreds of carloads of cattle came from Texas to be fattened on the luscious green grass and shipped to market in the fall.

A school of culture , led by Frank Frost, has sprung up which calls the Flint Hills the Bluestem Pastures, because "Flint Hills" sounds so barren, but they might as well try to name the Rocky Mountains the Evergreen Ridge.

Excuse me. Mr. Morrow wanted only to know where they were. Nobody asked me to run on like this. But now that you know, run down and see them sometime—preferably in June.

—September 13, 1936

*　　*　　*

Although her father may have let down in the last few months and reverted to greasy oil clothes and shapeless hats, Nancy Jo Landon has not yielded an inch in her defense of family prestige. One day she wanted a change of clothing, and while her mother told her her dress was all right, Nancy Jo looked her in the eye and said precisely, "Would you like to have it said that Mrs. Landon doesn't keep her children looking nice?"

—May 19, 1937

*　　*　　*

Nineteen years ago we thought we had made the world safe for democracy, but today we know it is not safe for anything. Another cycle of bloodshed is spinning itself out and another crop of boys is being fed to the war machine.

The talk twenty years ago sounded much like the talk today. It was said then that if Germany conquered France and England she would be over here next, and that sooner or later we would have to fight her, the presumption being that once Germany was fought and conquered, she would lie down to lick her wounds and be out of the way for all time.

Which is something like what is being said of Japan.

So we went ahead and whipped Germany. But did she settle down meekly after the chastisement of the Versailles Treaty?

She wasted little time licking her wounds. Suffering from hurt pride and humiliation, she smarted under the sting of defeat and was more than ever determined to have a place in the sun. Perhaps Germany is stronger today than she was before the war.

15

If we learned nothing else from the war, we should at least have learned the futility of fighting. You can't be sure, just because you force a player out of the game in the first quarter, that he won't come back in the last half stronger than before.

—November 11, 1937

Wanted—A Home

Nature has manifested itself again and Boots has become a mother. The childen, four of them, have been named Overshoes, Galoshes, Slippers, and Sandals, tho they are so nearly alike we can't tell Overshoes from Galoshes or Slippers from Sandals.

Their coming has created a problem, the vexing problem of what to do with four cunning little black and gray kittens. They frisk about the house so innocently and trustingly and their mother is so confident of their loving care—she watches them playing and looks at us proudly, as tho to say, "See what I have given you"—that we feel cruel and inhuman monsters to think of parting the happy family.

But the mathematical law of increasing series applied to cats makes it appallingly certain even to tearful Dorothy Anne that the kittens must go.

We are determined on one thing—they shall have good homes. They come of good stock. Boots was given us by a prominent local artist, and while nothing definite can be said about the father, still, the irreproachable good taste and impeccable judgment of Boots is guarantee enough of the refinement and gentility of the other side of the house.

Boots' children will not enter new homes as pensioners. With each will go a dowry of a can of salmon and a bottle of milk, assurances of the gentle dignity of their positions.

We could not think of allowing the kittens to go into uneducated homes. A college diploma might not be essential, but we shall insist that the family must have a good grasp of world conditions and a liberal and progressive viewpoint. They must take a good daily newspaper—preferably the local morning paper—and a number of thought-provoking and stimulating periodicals. The presence of sensational and trashy magazines in the home would react most unfavorably for the applicants.

We shall not insist, either, that the family be Republicans, as we know full well that there are a number of honest, worthy Democrats and some fathead Republicans. Rather shall they be judged by their intrinsic individual worth and sterling integrity. A well-behaved and clean-shaven Socialist who can meet the other requirements will not be barred from the pleasure of possessing a kitten.

Even more important than the political beliefs of the family is their mental and moral stability. We do not make a point of church membership or insist on definite views on baptism and infant damnation, but evidence of a spiritual life, such as regular attendance at Sunday School, would be a strong recommendation. While we prefer a liberal religious

16

outlook, a fundamentalist who is sincere and well-meaning and charitable will receive consideration.

It will be necessary that the house to which a kitten goes contain adequate cubic feet and floor space for each member of the family, with proper ventilation, a suitable number of bathrooms, and plenty of soft rugs. Kittens adore rugs.

We would like to place them within a few blocks of our own home, so Dorothy Anne can take Boots to visit them at regular intervals. Adoptions will not be final until six months of satisfactory probation convinces us that the family is entirely worthy and respectable and will make responsible parents.

—May 21, 1938

Lucky Girl

The conversation has turned to grandma's day. The young married women, with only one child or none at all, with leisure for matinees and bridge, with electric appliances in their home, were sighing over her unenlightened condition.

One girl did not chime in with clucks of pity. She had earned her living in an office for the six or eight years she had been out of school, and it was her opinion that while grandma might not have had much freedom, might have had to work hard, still there were a lot of things she didn't have to worry about.

She didn't have to fret about choosing a career or getting a job, or keeping them after she got them. She expected to be supported, first by her father or her nearest male relative and later by her husband. And because grandma acknowledged her dependence on men, they rose nobly to the occasion and married her.

The modern girl who boasts that she can make her own living is likely as not taken at her word and allowed to do so. She is allowed to pay her share of the expenses of dating and is rewarded by being called a good sport. But frequently middle age finds her still in the office.

Grandma didn't have to worry whether her good-looking date was really divorced, as he said he was, or whether there might be a wife or two around to bring bigamy charges in case she married him.

Grandma didn't have to decide about the stand she would take on smoking and drinking. No lady in her day did either. She didn't worry over whether she would be a teetotaler, sip a little for social appearances, or discover her capacity and be a good fellow.

Neither did she have to wonder if her date would be in condition to take her home safely or whether there might be an accident, with her picture in the paper and her escort held for drunken driving.

Grandma's evening held little more excitement than a Virginia reel or touching hands over the family album, with an occasional hayride thrown in, but she didn't have to be at the office at 8 the next morning.

Nor did grandma worry about choosing and comparing. She knew she was destined for marriage, so she took the first nice man who offered himself and was spared the discovery, after dating a dozen years, that the twentieth is no better than the first.

When she was married she knew it was permanent, and while she could not nick grandpa for a bunch of alimony, she knew that he would not be absconding with the blonde stenographer, because there was no blonde stenographer.

Grandpa might let his eye roam, but he stayed hitched. Such as he was, she knew she had him for life.

Grandma could grow old comfortably. She had to wear three petticoats, but knew not the agony of keeping herself in chiffon hose. She was burdened with corsets, it is true, but she did not have to dye her hair, torture herself with a permanent, or have her face lifted.

Hips were appreciated in grandma's time and there was no need to roll on the floor or starve herself into a shadow to keep up with the procession.

Grandma was a lucky old girl.

—June 28, 1938

* * *

The Capital's city editor is a sober, sedate, steady, hard-working, temperate young man. I feel it necessary to explain this because a couple of ladies who had come in to bring a social item looked at each other and raised their eyebrows when he answered the phone one evening.

What he said was, "I can't take much more tonight. I'm tight already." He referred, not to his physical condition, but to the fact that he had about all the copy he could use for the paper.

—September 7, 1938

Football

Hitler has the ball, is headed toward the goal with an open field, and at this distance there seems likely to be no interference to a touchdown.

It won't be the last one either. Of course quarterback Hitler will have to pause besides, go into a huddle and plan the next play, but it will come, for the game is just starting.

The opponents have seen the big boys sitting on the benches and they're jittery. In the tumult of cheering they forget the glorious old days when they were the champions of Europe and brought home enough pennants to make half a dozen bedspreads for Grandmother Victoria.

"But this new fellow—he's got something. Whatever you may think of Hitler—and you probably think plenty—he is a genius, an evil genius." Doctor Maxwell, of Washburn College calls him.

Doctor Maxwell, recently returned from Europe, tells of how the German people sit silently in the beer gardens. Formerly they liked to carry on lively discussions of politics and government over their steins. But now they just sit. And if they do talk it is to comment on the weather, on the football team, or to ask each other if they do not think the band is excellent. But there is no talk of government.

Doctor Maxwell explained the German attitude by a story of a German writing to a cousin in the United States, who had asked what they thought of the government over there.

The cousin replied: "I like the government. My father likes the government, my mother likes the government, and my brothers and sisters like the government. Uncle John, whose funeral was Thursday, didn't like the government."

—September 24, 1938

Wagon Wheels at Night

The slow crunch of wagon wheels on a road at night awakens eager memories of the times that my father went to the mountains for wood.

It was when we first moved to the little town in Colorado where no timber grew on the flat surface of the valley but the slender gray-green willows that lined up opposite each other on the banks of irrigation ditches.

Early in the morning—and that meant around 3 o'clock—my parents arose and my mother prepared breakfast while my father fed and harnessed the horses.

The noise of dishes always drew us from our beds, where he had tried to sleep with one eye open, to share the great adventure of going to the mysterious mountains that looked to be just beyond the wheat field but were really miles and miles away.

His lunch packed–and my mother piled the bucket with our choicest food—the horses hitched to the wagon, the tools loaded, and my father was ready to start before the first pale mist of dawn. We all went out to open the gate and see him go.

We longed to go with him, but he said we would be too tired. So he set out alone and we listened to the wheels grinding on the gravel driveway as he went, with faith that the dawn would come.

He was never expected to return until long after dark. The chores were done in excited anticipation, supper eaten, and a good portion set back to keep warm for the traveler.

In the soft darkness of evening we sat on the porch and listened for the wagon, straining our ears to catch the first grinding of iron wheels in the distance.

And then it would come, faint and far away on the still night air, increasing with slow but regular crescendo. My mother would sigh in relief and go into the house to warm up the supper.

What rejoicing there was as he turned in at our gate. We ran out and helped unhitch the horses and as they ate, the harness was removed by the flickering light of a kerosene lantern.

And of course we must view the wood, rich gnarled pine, exciting cargo

19

from a strange thrilling land. Sometimes there would be odd rocks he had brought home for us, or queer plants.

While my father was eating and after the excitement had somewhat died down, my mother always said she was afraid a tree might have fallen on him or that he might have pitched over a cliff, or have cut himself with the ax.

What we children wanted to know was whether he had seen a deer, to hear about waterfalls, frisky little unafraid animals, the wonderful dams made by beavers, dank, pine covered slopes and swift clear streams.

Wagon wheels at night. I cannot hear them without feeling again the excitement and joy and suspense and relief of a trip to the mountains. And now they mean to me the heavy burdens, the willing sacrifice, the tender care and love that our father gave to us.

—October 7, 1938

*   *   *

There is always a bit of compensation in any situation. Word comes that the Germans will not allow the Jews to attend the annual charity drives.

—December 6, 1938

*   *   *

"If you're around forty, you're lucky," says an ad, "and if you're younger, so much the better." And I suppose if you've not been born yet, you can thank your lucky stars.

When people grow old they regret the fun they missed in their youth, but at the same time they keep advising the young to be more sober, earnest, and industrious, to cultivate piety, to cut out the fooling around and get down to hard work.

—December 8, 1938

*   *   *

If college is to be an all around development for young people, more attention should be paid to bringing every student to a good physical condition and teaching him to guard his health. Instead, they pick out a few brawny ones and concentrate the hysteria of the student body and the alumni on orgies in which they are likely to get their necks broken.

While I'm complaining I might as well beef about the ten cents they charge for a coke at a football game. People resent being asked to pay double the price of a drink just because the sellers have the drop on them.

—December 10, 1938

Smells

A woman was making a fuss about her young daughter's use of cheap perfumes. The girl owned half a dozen bottles of various shapes and sizes, labeled with such names as Temptation, Irresistible, Fascination, Night of Love, which she poured recklessly over herself in spite of the fact that they cost ten cents each, a whole week's allowance.

The mother was getting set for a comparison reaching back to that near mythical time when she was a girl, a comparison in which daughter always came off second best, when she was stopped by a wave of memories.

She remembered a little girl, a girl who also wore pigtails and who was not unlike her daughter in appearance except that the dress of the former came well below her knees and overlapped her heavy cotton stockings, beneath which long underwear bulged above high laced shoes.

That little girl loved smells too. But on the hilly farm where she lived there were no smells bought especially for smelling. Nor were there any in the little town where they traded eggs for sugar and coffee while the miller ground their wheat and corn.

But there were smells that delighted the small sensitive nostrils. They were kept, not on a dressing table, but in the pantry and on the medicine shelf. The girl would slip into the pantry and sprinkle lemon and vanilla extract over her clothes or dust cinnamon and allspice into her brown braids to make herself smell nice.

Other fascinating smells were mint and catnip and tomato vines, sage and the sharp tang of vinegar, but none of them could touch camphor. She remembered the ecstatic smell of a piece of camphor gum and wondered what chance a sissy synthetic odor like Irresistible would have against the racy penetrating pungency of camphor.

Then there was clove oil. Even the toothache was not unpleasant, treated with cotton saturated in clove oil. When the pain finally flickered and left she could not have said which was more healing, the properties of the clove oil or the stinging sweetness.

Now when her daughter descends the stairs smelling of strange scents, her short plaid skirt flapping against bare legs, no recognition of the odor emanating from her person is evidenced other than a faint tightening of the nostrils.

But as the door bangs behind her, her mother sighs and in that sigh there is pity for a little girl in a city who is passing up the piquant sharp reality of honest smells for artificial scents in silly little bottles.

—January 31, 1939

Just One of the Girls

About the time I was writing in this column what a youthful, fine-looking fellow William Ackworth is, he was saying in the Iola Register that I looked thirty years younger than he expected I would. He claims I led him on to tell his age, then was careful not to volunteer my own, about which he was "exceedingly curious." He hopes I will oblige.

Certainly, I have no objection whatever to Mr. Ackworth knowing my age, but I feel sure he would prefer an engaging problem in deduction to a bald recital of numbers. Here are a few statements around which he can form some equations involving X, the unknown.

Although by the table of vital statistics half of my life is over, the best, according to the poet, is yet to be.

I am confident that the society editor would refer to me as a young matron, perhaps even a charming young matron. I assure you that she has said it of even more elderly ladies.

Last Sunday in a strange Sunday School, the superintendent looked me over and said, "I guess you'll go in the young people's class." I was very well pleased but when I saw the class I wondered when they had been young.

The same day a man at the door called me Miss. The day before when I was down town with my nine-year-old daughter, an elderly gentleman to whom I was introduced complimented me on my beautiful granddaughter.

Dorothy Anne herself regards me as being of a mellow old vintage and keeps asking me to tell her more about the olden days. It would not surprise her in the least to learn that I went to school with General Grant, about whom she is learning at school.

On the other hand my son Willard thinks I am young enough to start early in the morning and tramp all over the Shunganunga Valley and still be fresh enough to run up and down the Horseshoe cliffs. Nor should it tire me to tuck the lunch under my arm and sling the coats over my shoulder as I am pulled from crag to crag.

I have seen clapboard shingles hewed from the forest, have watched trees being split into rails for a fence, have gone to the mill and seen our own wheat and corn ground and watched a shuttle flying through the warp of a carpet.

But that was in the Ozarks, where time is not in a hurry. On the other hand, I still like dolls and enjoy riding a bicycle. But I'd rather sit by the fire than build a snowman. The other day a man whom I do not see often exclaimed that I look younger every year.

With these few hints a bright person like Mr. Ackworth should have no trouble arriving at the correct figure, but to make it easier I will say that I am not customarily addressed as "auntie" or "granny" by strangers.

—March 2, 1939

* * *

A fifty-years-ago item tells of the arrest of a young man in a theater for disorderly conduct. He had one arm around a girl.

—April 27, 1939

Tennis

If baseball is a roughneck's game, tennis is the sport of gentlemen. There is such an air of conscious politeness around the courts that you half expect someone to hand you a cup of tea and pass a tray of those little cakes.

A swift tennis game is as nerve-tingling as a dance. Sweet parabolas, long slim curves, graceful volleys are accompanied by bodily motion that is beautiful because it is effective in speed and economy.

Even the spectators at a tennis game become gentlemen for the time. There is as much dignity and decorum per square foot as you would find at an undertaker's convention. No audible opinions are expressed concerning the players and the referee is not threatened with sudden death.

A fast serve comes over. You think it is good, but the referee calls it a ball. You turn to your companion and in the same voice with which you would express preference for lemon or cream, you say, "It seemed to be good, from up here, tho of course he can see much better from his position." Did you ever hear a spectator behind the diamond admit that the umpire might be better able to judge a point than himself?

The players are as polite to each other as social enemies meeting at a tea. Your opponent zips one right past you for whatever a Texas leaguer is called in tennis. You exclaim admiringly, "Nice shot!" and he returns the compliment when you smack the tape in the northeast corner.

When the game is ended the losers leap across the net to shake hands with and congratulate the winners, who in turn say what a stiff game it was and make pleasant remarks about the opponents' serve or backhand.

I don't remember whether they bow from the waist or curtsy as they leave each other, or maybe kiss as the French do.

The referee, too, is a gentleman and his word is good. No sultry looks or muttered rumblings, no players coming in from the backfield to contest a point. He refers to the players as "Mister," tho I have heard there is some sentiment for changing it to "Esquire."

A person who is a shrieking, yelling, primitive creature behind the diamond is transformed into a Lord Chesterfield beside the tennis courts. I do not understand it, but I wonder if the problems of nations might not be solved and the peace of the world maintained by a huge network of international tennis matches.

—July 5, 1939

A Personal Matter

The human animal when perplexed does some queer thinking. The last few years most of the state legislatures have introduced bills designed to keep married women from holding jobs. Men who aren't getting along blame women for taking employment from them, and unmarried women accuse their wedded sisters of selfish motives in seeking a paycheck.

A lady writes this column, "If every married woman in Topeka would resign her job and let the married men and college boys get in, there would be happy homes for all and the Government would not need to have relief for any."

The theory is vulnerable at every point. In the first place it is based on a false premise, the one that every job now held by a woman would be available to a man at a salary on which he could raise a family.

Such is not the case. Hundreds of women are working for wages on which one could barely live decently. If those wages were increased, prices would rise. If they were not, the standard of living would go down. In either case, the economic balance would be disturbed.

The point of the whole matter is extremely simple. Women have always worked. There has never been a time in the world when the efforts of the man alone could support a family. Women have always contributed to the material welfare of the family. Formerly it was done in the home. Now the machine age has moved it to the factory. But women still have to work. In going out to find jobs they are merely adjusting themselves to new conditions.

Holding to the theory that every able individual, including women, must contribute some kind of work in return for a living, it seems senseless to haggle about what kind of work and where and in what marital condition it is done.

It is stupid and presumptuous for legislators to consider bills setting forth the condition of married women and single women, defining what each may or may not do.

Marriage is a personal, private matter, but women are women, whether married or single.

Whether a woman irons a shirt in her own home or in a laundry, it is work, and whether she runs a sweeper or an adding machine, she is contributing to the general welfare. There are certain tasks which must be performed. It doesn't matter in the long run who does what, if all get done.

Every wife who works outside her home creates employment — for maids, nurses, laundresses, cleaners, music and art teachers—in addition to stimulating business with her increased buying power.

I am certain the lady means well, but I doubt that even the men would appreciate having her suggestion taken literally. The little woman's pay check makes life easier and pleasanter for her husband, relieves him of financial worries and gives him a breathing spell. It enables the family to have a piano, a car, to send children to college, and take care of dependent relatives.

Industry has accepted the woman worker because she does some things better than men and others more cheaply. It would be hard to picture schools, hospitals, beauty parlors, stores, and even offices, run satisfactorily without women workers.

Those who want women to step aside in favor of their brothers surely do not expect a man to raise and educate a family on the wages received by the average woman worker. They apparently assume that the wages for that particular job will be doubled or tripled and business will go on as usual.

That is only the economic aspect. The personal is even more important, from a theoretical view. Her own circumstances and desires, her ambition and ability, should be the issues in a woman's decision to take a job. Not all married women want to work outside their homes. I believe that a great majority of women and girls prefer a home and housework and family to a job. They take the job because they need the money.

I personally feel that it is highly desirable for a mother to remain at home and take care of her children and that society will suffer if she is forced out to get a job. Creating a haven of peace and happiness for her family is the work at which most women excel.

But a woman must work, somewhere, and she and her husband are the ones to decide whether she can contribute more to the family by working in the home or by taking a job. It is a personal matter, not one for legislatures.

—October 17, 1939

No Great Hurry

I have come to the conclusion that there is no great hurry about winning fame and wealth and ease. I am beginning to learn that the pinnacle of success is only a point from which the attainer looks back and sighs for the wonderful days when he had to struggle and fight and wrestle for the bread he ate.

Taking it from those who should know, the struggling days are the best days. So why should anybody wish them to end?

I know a man who has acquired success in business and politics. He has done a lot of whickering and maneuvering in his day, big deals which should make elegant conversation. But if you talk to him for more than ten minutes he will get around to the winter he herded sheep in the mountains, alone and it was forty below zero. It is the biggest he-man job he ever did and he is more proud of it than of the coup which defeated a Governor.

Those who look back wistfully on the good old days are in reality looking back to good old youth. A man who was arguing the other day for a return to hard work and plain living is one who struggled endlessly in his youth to have something more than that meager fare.

All the time he was wearing patched overalls and eating potatoes and corn bread (the best food on earth) he was planning for the day when they could move to town, take it easy, and let mamma send out the washing.

Now he mistakes his vigorous years for the conditions of those years. He knows that the good days were when the battle of life was fierce and lusty and when he rejoiced as a strong man for the conflict.

I wonder if the old fellows living in 1980 will talk about the hardships of 1940, when only the rich could own airplanes and spend winters in Florida, and when houses were hot in summer and cold in winter.

This is a prophecy. Paste it in your bombproof scrapbook and look at it in 1980.

—January 11, 1940

* * *

A deep conviction of guilt and a sense of shame smote me when Dorothy Anne came home from a neighbor's all excited.

"Beverly's mother is making a quilt," she announced. "She takes two pieces of cloth and puts cotton between them, then she sews them together. Mother, you must come over and see it."

I groveled under the unconscious reproach. Oh, that a child of mine should be driven from home to learn the facts of life in regard to the putting together of a simple, homely comforter! 'Twere better that I had stayed at home and tacked one of the things rather than bought blankets in the after-Christmas sales.

O, the times! O, the customs!

—February 6, 1940

Woman's Work

I wonder if Hester Potter hasn't stumbled on to something pretty significant. Hester, who lives on a farm in Brown County, was left several years ago with the farm to manage, including a herd of beef cattle.

Before that time Hester had been given the chickens to take care of, chickens being considered women's work. After several years of farm experience on her own, Hester thinks it's no more work to take care of a herd of Whitefaces than a flock of chickens, and lots more fun.

You know how it is. Breakfast over some fine morning you say that you've simply got to clean out the henhouse. The man of the family rises hastily, before a hint can be dropped that you could use a little help, and, trying to sound like a martyr, guesses he'll have to ride out to the pastures this morning and see that the cattle have salt and that the fences are all right. Can't afford to let any of those cattle get away, no sir.

You get yourself up in an outfit that makes you look like a Russian refugee, tie an old bandana about your head, don canvas gloves, and tackle the poultry house. You shovel and scrape and lift until your back screams in rebellion.

In the meantime the cattle tender is trotting along thru green pastures and beside still waters, whistling a gay aria. He draws his lungs full of fresh pure air, looks up at the fleecy clouds flecking the blue, blue sky, and concludes that life is good.

The cattle are grazing peacefully, they have plenty of salt, and the fence posts are supporting their strings as bravely as the bridge of a violin.

The man sees a neighbor out in his field and rides over to chat about the new Farm Bureau officers and other things, including a few juicy mouthfuls of local happenings. And so home in time for dinner, which his wife left her chicken house cleaning to prepare. If a question of the day's occupation ever arises he can say he was "out all morning looking after those cattle."

Hester declares what many of you have long suspected, that riding around in the pastures looking after cattle is fun. Men like to do it, so they created the legend that it is hard work. They know that chickens are a drudgery and a darned nuisance. So they are women's work.

Women are the drudges in the business world not so much because of their inferior strength as their emotional habits.

Very few women can completely shed the age-long tradition of domestic responsibility. The Indian woman tended the maize while her brave was off hunting and dressed the meat when he returned.

—February 10, 1940

Every Emotion

"Really," said a neighbor, returning from seeing "Gone With the Wind," you must see it. It's perfectly wonderful. You feel every emotion there is, every one."

That's all I needed. I made up my mind that moment. I don't need to tell you that emotions can come pretty high. Many a lady has paid dearly for them. So when one is guaranteed that she can experience every emotion for only 75 cents—well, it's like Dollar Day, Odds and Ends Sale, and an Anniversary Jubilee all in one. Right there I decided to invest three quarters of a dollar in emotions.

And what a six bits' worth! The lady was right, absolutely right. They rolled over you, submerged you, encompassed you, clutched you, gripped and tore you, stifled you, and before one emotion could be classified, catalogued, and quieted, another was upon you.

Persons who had read the lengthy novel told you smugly, "I've read the book and I'm glad I did. I got so much more out of the picture."

The nonreaders were equally complacent. I'm certainly thankful I didn't read the book," they told any who were interested and some who were not. "I enjoyed the picture so much more than if I knew everything that was going on."

I am in favor of a law compelling persons going into such a show to wear a muzzle. If any of the plot was still unknown after the numerous reviews, it was broadcast in loud whispers thru the audience.

"She's going to be killed pretty soon," a woman in the next seat would volunteer, right after the one just ahead had sighed that she loses him in the end."

While I would have been pleased to have discovered a few of those things myself, it wasn't necessary. I got my money's worth from the generation of emotions, which at times threatened to exceed the capacity of human storage batteries. There was no time to weep and the extra handkerchiefs were not needed. The time went swiftly, like the seven years Jacob labored for Rachel, which "seemed unto him but a few days, for the love he had to her."

This column has never been among the Clark Gable fans. We go for

27

Charles Boyer and Gary Cooper, not for the leering Gable grin. But now—could you move along a bit, girls, and make room for me?

As Rhett Butler, Clark Gable was perfect. One of the finest parts of the play was the magnificent, but amusing determination of Rhett that his beloved baby daughter should grow up and be accepted by the best people, by whom he himself was not overly esteemed.

He wheeled the baby on the streets, bowing and smiling deferentially to all the important women he met. He consulted them eagerly on baby-tending, begging cures for thumbsucking, until he won them completely. One has a sneaking suspicion that the respectable old dowagers were entranced by his devilish smile and charming manners, but their capitulation was put on the grounds that a man who loved a child so dearly could not be entirely bad.

What a joy it must have been to Margaret Mitchell to see Vivien Leigh bring Scarlett to glowing, vibrant life right before her eyes. Surely it was one picture that pleased the author.

It's going to be pretty hard now to enjoy ordinary films about ordinary people made by ordinary methods, after seeing Scarlett and Rhett and Melanie and Ashley Wilkes in their beautiful and terrible conflicts.

—March 4, 1940

Mortgagor and Mortgagee

If this column has seemed to lack clarity or logic, in recent days, it has been because of the moving. Last Saturday the van transferred our worldly goods to our newly acquired house. Or, I should say, most of our worldly goods. We have been going back for additional junk every day since.

Sweet words—our own house—"to have and to hold, together with all and singular the tenements, hereditaments, and appurtenances thereunto belonging, and the rents, issues, and profits thereof."

That's what it says in the papers that came with it. And more—we may also have and hold forever all the "chattels, mantels, elevators, awnings, and all other fixtures now or hereafter standing on said real estate."

So I take it that the house is ours, and the patch of ground surrounding it, clear down the 4,000-mile apex to the core of the earth and all that is contained therein, now and forever, and we can expect to be standing in the front door looking out when Gabe blows the whistle and ends the game.

I noticed all summer that my husband seemed restless, sort of lost-like. He sighed and stared into space and talked about taking up wood-working.

My womanly instinct told me he needed a mortgage.

Out on the farm we always had a mortgage and were perfectly happy. But last spring we sold the farm and my husband had nothing to worry about except what he would do with the $200 equity he obtained from the transaction.

First thing we knew we had no debts. That was when my husband began to go to pieces. I can see it now.

Love is all right in moderation, and companionship has its place, but there's nothing like a mortgage to keep a man zooming along at top speed, content with the world.

Three months before the semiannual payments are due he is scraping together every cent to meet the interest. So he has no time to be fussy or restless, and for three months' afterwards he is too happy to be.

With a brand new mortgage my husband is his old sweet self again.

A mortgage is a magnificent piece of work. It rolls along in a thundering majesty positively scriptural.

To wit, "And the mortgagor covenants with the mortgagee that he is lawfully seized in fee of the premises hereby conveyed. . . as aforesaid, and will warrant and defend the title thereto forever against the claims and demands of all persons whomsoever."

A mortgage is as thrilling as a fire engine and as final as the judgment day. Too bad the author is modestly anonymous.

Written the evening of the third day.

—November 7, 1940

* * *

Christmas giving loses its joyful significance when you have to rack your brains to think of something that will please a finicky recipient, and something she doesn't already have.

A woman said the other day, "I'm getting tired of shopping for adults. Christmas is no fun since the nieces and nephews have grown up."

Last minute Christmas shopping is a sport that the prissies who have everything wrapped by Labor Day know nothing about.

How can they know the thrill of buying the very last beautiful jeweled leather bracelet when they picked laconically from the entire stock?

Theirs is not the sweet breathless wonder of waiting while the clerk rummages in the stockroom to see if they might possibly have another collared flannel nightie size 44.

And their smug complacence is a pitiful substitute for the wild delight your racing heart registers when the clerk takes the last singing teakettle from the window and wraps it up for you.

—December 19, 1940

II
1941-1949

In former days, I am told, common citizens were awed by Congressmen and ill at ease in their presence. Nobody wanted to be left alone very long with one of them for fear of being embarrassed by the knowledge and wisdom of the great man.

Once when a member of Congress was making a visit to a small Kansas town the citizenry was flustered for lack of a smart conveyance to haul the eminent one around in.

Then somebody thought of Old Henry out north of town. Henry couldn't read nor write, he made a cross to sign his name, and he wouldn't have known whether Congress was a new kind of riding skirt for women or one of those sliding things you looked at colored pictures thru.

The very thing, sighed the county chairman, almost collapsing with relief. Henry's one indulgence and his pride and joy was his fine team of horses and his slick new buggy.

Only two could ride in a buggy and since the Congressman was a well-padded gentleman, Henry went alone to the depot to meet the pillar of wisdom and drive him to the city hall.

"What did you talk about?" they asked Henry with new respect for his poise and assurance in the presence of greatness.

"We didn't talk about much o' nothin'," said Henry. "He 'lowed he was goin' to make a talk and I said I didn't never go to no speakin's. Then I gave him a chaw of tobaccer and we just kind of jogged along."

—July 25, 1941

31

Press Conference

Probably nowhere in the world can one see a more interesting exhibition of poise than in President Roosevelt's press conferences. There for eight years, going on nine, he has faced his critics on the mound, right handers and left, Bob Fellers, spit and curve ballers, umpired only by the unwritten code known as newspaper ethics.

Twice a week the press gathers in a reception room in the executive wing of the White House and throw their hats on the big round table supported by carved wooden calves' heads. As the hour approaches they gather around the door thru which they will be admitted, as determined on holding their places as a woman waiting for a store to open on bargain day.

At last the word is given and the press hurries in and crowds around the President's big desk in the oval room, a desk that is littered with all kinds of trinkets.

For a minute the President gives no sign that the mob has thundered in. He continues to look thru his papers. When he does speak it is without looking up, without formal greeting, and in the tone of one who takes up a conversation that has been momentarily interrupted.

Mr. Roosevelt looks older and more weary than he did six years ago, but who of us does not? His white shirt carries a red and blue monogram on the sleeve, matched by a red and blue plaid tie, and his trousers are of a sort of gray seersucker. With fingers not as steady as they used to be he picks up and lays down the cigarette in the long holder, which he smokes from time to time.

The Roosevelt smile may not be quite as spontaneous as in less troubled days, but it still has its old charm. It can be used, too, as a woman's, to cover up feelings he wishes to hide. The President blows out his cheeks and puckers up his mouth when he is considering an answer to a question.

When Mr. Roosevelt replies that he considers no comment necessary, as he did to the suggestion that he comment on the Willkie statement about our establishing bases in Ireland, it is a new definition of finality.

Some of the more seasoned correspondents, not lacking in poise themselves, do not hesitate to interrupt and disagree, politely, of course, but the President never lacks for an answer. At times there is a hint of sharpness in his voice, or of wariness, and when a question that was meant to lead him into embarrassing discussion is answered with frank candor to the effect that he doesn't know, as tho the query was a matter of no importance whatever, there is just nothing more to be said. The old maestro has closed the subject.

—July 26, 1941

Freedoms

The frenzied joy of the first Armistice will nowhere be echoed this day. Rather will the anniversary recall the tragedy of that struggle twenty-five years ago and bring the despairing wonder if it will mean a new war every quarter of a century.

I have been interested in trying to determine public opinion in regard to the present situation and have been bringing up the question as I talk with people from day to day.

What I find is confusion—in high places and low. For every person who speaks out with clear-cut decisiveness, there are nine others with whom vague generalities and sentimental wishing pass for thinking.

Everybody wants Hitler stopped, but they don't want a war. They favor aid to England, but will not say how much or of what it should consist.

The truth is that few people are able to pursue a question to its relentless conclusion and face what lies at the end. They are like a little girl I know who desires many things earnestly, if her parents will buy them, but there are few things she wants bad enough to spend her own precious bank account, saved in pennies from her small allowance.

Today might be a good time to sit down and think the thing thru. It will have little effect on actual events, but to clarify one's own mind is valuable.

What are the probabilities if we send men across, win the war, and undertake to dispense the four freedoms? On the other hand, what are the likely conditions if we do not? We ought to be sure that what we buy is worth what it will cost, and you may be sure it will amount to a pretty penny.

—November 11, 1941

Sunday Afternoon

At first I thought it was a gag on a Sunday evening radio program—something about somebody bombing Honolulu—then it struck with swift suddenness that it was no comedian's jest, but war.

It may be a Sunday afternoon long to be remembered. The Preston Hales invited us to their farm to gather black walnuts and we planned to take wienies and cook over an outdoor fire.

A December sun was never more mellow than Sunday afternoon. Wood was gathered and a fire built between two rocks, everybody wanting to strike the match. Coats came off as the dry wood began to crackle and fill the air with smoke.

We roasted wienies on long sticks, broiled steak the same way or laid it on the coals, fried potatoes that had already been boiled, and ate with grand unconcern for dirt and ashes. We forgot the butter, but nobody cared. We had salt and pepper and a big dill pickle.

In faded slacks, old coat, warm stockings, peasant scarf, and cotton work gloves, there was no need to worry about snags or runners or cold,

33

and my host failed to make me mad when he said I ought to be taken down into the hills of Arkansas and turned loose.

It was deeply satisfying to lie on the sunny slope and squint at the blue sky thru a network of laced trees, to breathe in long gusts of air tanged with wood smoke, and wander in fancy to Timbuktu and Guatemala, steeped in pure, childish, carefree happiness.

We picked up walnuts and gathered wood for the fireplace, we loitered in the woods and put off our return as long as possible, then drove home slowly past Lake Shawnee and stopped to watch the flocks of wild ducks floating on its surface and rising to dot the crimson flame of the sunset.

We must come again, we told each other.

Yes, indeed. Every Sunday. Well, anyway, often.

At home unloading the wood and walnuts and feeling like real farmers again, then into the house at 6 o'clock and turning on our favorite radio program.

All the time we had been looking at the blue Kansas sky, death was flashing thru the blue skies of Hawaii, dark bombers making a network like bare tree limbs and blood staining the water like a crimson sunset.

Bit by bit it was coming out of the radio—war. We sat in silence while the fire burned out and the newsboys' "Extra" shattered the crystal night air.

Then our boy coming to us, tall and sweet and young, "Mom, I'd like to be a flier in the Army, or maybe the Navy would be better." Only sixteen, I was thinking, and as if guessing my thoughts, "Heck, I bet I could pass for eighteen."

But there were boys eighteen, twenty, twenty-two, and tomorrow they might be going up to the recruiting stations. Haven't boys always gone when there was a war?

Now that it has come there is shuddering relief from the torture of uncertainty. And there is national unity where yesterday one way of thinking was squared against another way. Now all stand together to work, to sacrifice, to suffer, to die that our country may be preserved.

Perhaps there will never be a moral equivalent of war.

—December 10, 1941

Three Women

A new generation of women is learning about war.

The other day in a Kansas town west of Fort Riley a woman was having her hair done. The operator, a slim, pale girl, was preoccupied and uninterested, seeming not to care whether her customer's back hair was rolled under or over. With difficulty the woman restrained herself from speaking sharply to the girl.

Then the phone rang. The girl dropped a handful of hairpins and let a nice wave sag out of place. Answering that phone was the first thing the woman had seen her attend to with an enthusiasm.

34

It was not until later that she learned the call had been from the girl's soldier sweetheart, who was traveling west with a motor caravan from Fort Riley. He couldn't stop long enough to see her, but had promised to phone her if he could.

It was their only good-by.

In the same town an Army officer's wife sits in traveling clothers with packed bags, afraid to leave her room, for she expects any day to have a call from her husband that he is being sent to the coast and she's going too. She has had some training as a nurse and she knows she can find something to do that will help.

In a local store a smiling woman waited on the crowds of Christmas shoppers Saturday. She looked happy and gay, yet when I spoke to her she told me her boy had left that morning to join the air service and she didn't see how she could get thru the day. He was nineteen and had gone away in the gray chill of dawn.

—December 17, 1941

* * *

William Allen White motioned me into the littered cubbyhole of his office and waved me to a seat. The conversation brought out that he was planning to write some Recollections of a Foolish Life.

"Are you going to put them into a book?" I asked.

"Well," indignantly, "you don't think I could get them on a postcard, do you?"

It was about nine years ago that I first visited Mr. White in his office, which today looks not one bit different. No doubt the books now piled high on top of his desk are of a later vintage and the letters bear a more recent postmark, but desk, office, books, chairs, papers, Mr. White himself, who is as pink and cherubic as the first time I saw him, look as tho the magic wand had been waved over all, ordaining that change here should cease, that this charming spot of friendliness should remain forever as it is.

—December 18, 1941

Voluntary Discipline

If Hitler or anybody else counted on our country being weak and ineffectual because of the violence of disagreement among ouselves in time of peace, he is due for a shock.

No nation could react more effectively under restraint than the United States. And that is because the restraint will be, in effect, voluntary. No Gestapo will need to silence radios, to snoop at doors, to open mail, or whisk good citizens away to concentration camps.

The restrictions are already under way and more will be coming. Many of them may seem ridiculous and unnecessary and some will be, but our people will understand that they are considered vital for the common good and they will be respected and observed without complaint.

35

I'm thinking particularly of the Kansas editors, than whom no class of persons on this troubled sphere are more militantly independent and jealous of their freedom.

They fight among themselves continually, about elections and taxes, about pawpaws and persimmons, about domestic and foreign policies, about pumpkin pie, Indian summer, frock coats, and falling hair.

This enthusiastic disagreement, carried into national affairs and multiplied over the forty-eight states, has apparently led ambitious despots to believe that Americans would accommodate them by eating each other up should we become engaged in a war.

Yet these Kansas editors, as editors and people everywhere, are accepting without a murmur the restrictions already imposed—the curtailment of weather reports, the omission of news concerning troop movements. The importance of unified action and the necessity of central authority are recognized and will be obeyed, even tho, like the famed Light Brigade, we may know at times that somebody has blundered. Nobody can be right all the time.

A free people are accustomed to restrictions which are voluntarily undertaken. We enjoy hunting and fishing, but we limit ourselves to certain periods and observe certain regulations so that there may be hunting and fishing next year and the next.

The game wardens could not possibly enforce these laws if the great majority of persons did not understand that it is to their interest to obey them.

The foundation of a democracy lies in the intelligent self-interest of the people willingly to accept the regulations imposed by their elected officials. And in time of war that self-interest is cemented into a strong and impregnable unity.

But when it's all over, when the enemy is silenced, then old differences will again be aired and type will sizzle under burning invective about whipped cream and fruit salad.

Freedom of speech, freedom of the press, will not have been lost. They may need partially and voluntarily to be curtailed, but they will return, or holy hell will break out that will make Pearl Harbor forgotten.

Our job now is to do whatever needs to be done. We will go without sugar, without hairpins, without zippers, and will even learn to walk again when tires are worn out. And we'll do so willingly, gladly, voluntarily, as we know what is needed.

No discipline is so effective as that which is self-imposed.

—January 1, 1942

Valentine Blitzkrieg

At early dawn your tramping hordes thundered
Into my heart—You said it was protective custody—and plundered.
Vain to struggle! And since you have declared priority
And absolute totalitarian authority

36

And set your foot to still my palpitation,
You might as well move in for the duration.
And while it's too late now to have the situation mended.
They say the fortress was inadequately defended.
Surely no invader could so soon have pried
The gates, unless unbolted first inside.

—February 14, 1942

*   *   *

Each year when April "shakes out her rain-drenched hair" we go about saying we never saw the flowers so beautiful. It's almost true this year.

Have flowering shrubs ever before been so heavy with bloom, so reckless with color, so lusciously abundant?

There is one pleasant association this spring with the name "Japan"—the Japan quince, or japonica, that sturdy pioneer shrub with its rose-red blossoms peeping out from the green leaves like shy children.

The Japanese people have a deep love for flowers and are famous for their arrangement. Perhaps the sight of a blossom on the stem is gladdening their hearts this April, for their sons and husbands too are at war and they too suffer grief and deprivation.

—April 20, 1942

*   *   *

Western Kansas is wearing its blond hair in the new victory cut, the same length all over its head. It ripples in a tender breeze or is whipped into a tangled mat of gold when a heavy wind lays itself across the earth. And spread under the arched drier of the sun after a shampoo of rain, the glistening waves are something to put in a magazine.

But the new modishness is brief. Already the heavy shears are at work and the golden glory is falling, leaving only the stiff, stubby ends of a clipped head.

Standing as proudly as new soldiers on sentry are the little clusters of shining grain bins dotting the western part of the state and waiting to receive the tumbling cascade of wheat.

—July 3, 1942

Boys

The world does not do right by boys. Their needs are ignored and neglected, yet when danger comes, they are the first pushed out to hold it off.

Every effort is made to see that girls are nurtured gently into bud and blossom and protected from blight, but who does anything to smooth a boy's life?

Prophecies

Prophecies for the future are springing up like weeds after rain (a magazine called "Predictions" is in its third number) and they seem to fall as easily and copiously as the rain itself.

It may prove that the stout heart and valiant soul of man looks to the bright future when days are darkest, but more likely it is an escape from the mistakes of the past and the realities of the present. Even so, it beats crossword puzzles.

Here are some necks stuck out:

We can beat Japan by 1946.

Germany will scatter cholera and bubonic germs in her last desperate stand.

Russia will turn to capitalism, China to Communism. India will gain freedom.

Within ten years no human living today will recognize the United States, says Predictor Walter Pitkin. (Who would recognize it now from ten years ago?)

Concrete ships, guided by radio, will sail across the ocean without a man on board and will mend its leaks automatically.

Planes will carry 400 passengers across the ocean. Gasoline will be 100 per cent more powerful. Cars will be amphibian.

Large comfortable hotels and solid landing fields will be built in the middle of the ocean.

Synthetic tires will run 100,000 miles.

Dehydrated food will replace canned.

Clothes will shed water. Sheer stockings cannot be made to run.

Girls will admire themselves in mirrors, and preen in new dresses.

Boys will tear three-cornered holes in their pants and bring home stray dogs.

Farmers will inspect crops on sunshiny mornings.

There will be sighing in May at the sweet sad notes of the turtle dove.

Men will hurry thru work to go fishing.

The big ones will get away.

Mothers will scold because potato peelings are thick.

Women will glance into dark store windows and catch up a wisp of hair.

Neighbors will meet in backyards and say how nice the lilacs are this year.

A boy will lie on a hillside and dream.

Women will close their eyes when being kissed.

Children will run outdoors at the first snow.

Editors will slip home after dark the day the paper comes out so not to meet the man whose name was spelled wrong.

Husbands and wives will not agree on the amount of cover needed on a bed.

A man will put on his hat and go to the barn when he is mad at his wife.
People will say things and be sorry they were said.
Men will boast about the hay they pitched.
A boy and girl will fall in love and think nobody ever loved before.
A woman will go to the orchard and return with apples in her skirt.
Children will want to be tucked in bed by their mothers and told about the three bears.
Leaves turning color and falling will cause a gentle melancholy.
A vain tinkling woman will bring sorrow to a man.
Women will strive for beauty, men will scheme for power, and for the same reason—to be desirable in each others' eyes.
People will climb to the top of a hill and look down.
When spring comes, men will turn the earth and plant.
Women will weep and not be able to give a reason.
Maidens will know when to be modest and when to be bold.
Many will sigh on the moon and love rain on the roof.
Women will sniffle at weddings.
Wind in the trees will bring strange feelings.
Your own loved ones safe around your own hearth will be counted by the wise as the greatest riches.
These things will be whether we live in houses that open by a radio beam or a door that scrapes, whether we travel by cart or seven-motored plane, whether our dress sheds water or catches lint, whether we are warmed by smoky stoves or sunray heaters.
These things will be.

—May 22, 1943

Common People

It is the fashion for certain self-styled intellectuals to sneer at the common people—the people, they say, who form mobs, burn witches, elevate the stupid to office, slide thru a groove their life long, put up with shallow sentiment and call it thinking.

All of which is true as charged, if you look at only one side. The masses are indifferent and unaware of their power and possibilities.

The bulk of the people have to expend most of their energy merely to live and have been slow to express themselves on matters of policy. There is among them a mild and good-humored cynicism to the effect that one set of officials is about as bad as another.

Rosy propaganda by the party in power, plus mass condemnation by their opponents has contributed to this attitude. Just how, the common man asks himself, can one know the truth with both sides painting their own bright pictures.

But when trouble comes it is the common man who frees the world from the blundering of its leaders.

Common men fight the wars that statesmen did not prevent, they rise

41

The act was shocking and should be resented. But the general has been reprimanded and has made amends. The stinging criticism, the loss of respect, has no doubt been bitter punishment to "Old Blood and Guts" for his arrogance.

Why not let the matter rest and get on with the war? Someone has said that he who is passionate and honest can be trusted. Perhaps even a general should be allowed a few mistakes. Everybody else is.

It is even more regrettable that the army headquarters put themselves in a hole by flatly and firmly denying the whole story, then later admitting it was true. It has hurt them with the people and shaken confidence in future dispatches.

For the people to know whatever happens, even the unfortunate things, and discuss them freely, not sparing those in high places, is the precious privilege of a democracy. If it is worth fighting for, it is worth practicing.

—November 27, 1943

Christmas Is a Good Time

That is the way Dorothy Anne summed it up when the first plans were being made.

She had in mind the glitter and gaiety of a modern child's Christmas and I thought how dull she would consider my childhood holidays on a hilly Missouri farm. There were no decorated trees, no candles or baubles, no beribboned packages.

The general store did not go in for tinsel and glitter. Christmas shopping was not something that one was reminded there were only so many days left for. Along in December our parents hitched up to the wagon and drove to town where they traded eggs and butter for candy and nuts and a few simple toys.

One Christmas deep in my memory is the one I got the little iron. We hurried out of bed and ran in long underwear to the warmth of the old box heater, getting under way with the roar of a B-17. The smell of cooking food came into the "big room," which was not big at all.

There were the nuts and candy, a small China silk handkerchief with the print of a quaint little girl in one corner, but not more quaint or queer than the one that received it. And there was the iron, a tiny one pointed at both ends and with a twisted handle.

It was moved to Colorado and later I took it to my home in Kansas. I fancied my own daughter cherishing it, but she gave it the cool inspection due an old-fashioned curiosity. What she wanted was a little electric iron that would heat and a folding ironing board.

But it was shared with other gifts and was not the focal point of joy my iron had been. Thirty-odd years ago seemed another era.

Sitting in that plain little room, with the coal oil lamp pinning shadows

44

against the wall, eating candy and nuts, feeling the softness of the silk and curling my fingers around the handle of the iron, I knew a deep abiding joy.

Christmas is a good time.

—December 25, 1943

*   *   *

One thing to be said for 1943—it helped some people get over allergies and what-have-you. Several persons discovered they could eat about anything the ration book would provide.

Others found that the woman next door whose son was in the South Pacific, seemed to lose interest in their nervous symptoms, and when they stopped talking about them, they seemed to lose the symptoms.

—December 30, 1943

The Loneliness

The prairies of Kansas are long and wide, even today when their expanse is broken by brisk towns with tall elevators and water towers, with farmhouses and schools.

To the pioneer whose own little dugout was the only man-made mark within the horizon's circle, they must have seemed endless.

In 1876 a Civil War veteran named Cassidy moved from West Virginia to Reno County with his wife and four little girls, aged three to ten. They were welcomed by the grasshoppers, who helped themselves to Cassidy's first crop.

It left them destitute. They had nothing to live on, nothing to take them back home.

Mr. Cassidy tried to borrow money in Hutchinson, but failed wherever he asked. The winter threatened them like an iceberg standing out suddenly in a fog.

About then a letter came and in it was fifteen dollars a man had borrowed several years before. The borrower apologized, but Mr. Cassidy blessed his debtor's delay.

The question was not, could they live a year on fifteen dollars. It was: What will fifteen dollars buy?

No marooned soldiers rationed their supplies more carefully. The Cassidys decided they could not buy flour or sugar. They had a cow and some of the canned fruit they had brought with them. Cornmeal and sorghum was what they ate. Their only fuel was buffalo chips.

The little girls' shoes were soon worn out and they went barefoot all winter. On sunny days they would sit on top of the dugout and watch the bands of Indians, the wagons and men on horseback that went along Sun City trail a mile away.

Involved in Mankind

Encouraged by manufacturers and advertisers, the people of this country are taking a trip on a magic carpet into the fairyland of good things to come after the war.

Houses, food, clothing, transportation—all are being touched with wands and wishing rings.

And one must not forget man himself. Nor his little woman. With vitamins to keep her hair from turning gray, face creams treated with preservatives, and cyclone-sifted powder, mamma will be as young and pretty as a Hollywood chorus girl, and papa will hardly bother to turn on the television when Miss Atlantic City is crowned.

It sounds fine, but it may take a little time to bring about.

I am not skeptical of the scientists and inventors. They are always far ahead of the economists, chiefly because they do not have to concern themselves with the muddling of mankind, but only with pure facts.

The world will wake up the morning after, not to a golden age, but to hurricane destruction. It will see, in the cold dawn, ruined cities, impoverished nations, shock-dulled people, disease and malnutrition, and the most staggering war debt the world has ever faced.

Groups will struggle for power as never before. There will be the wounded, broken families, depleted materials, and taxes and more taxes for Government compensations of all kinds.

And talk and shouting and tumult around the clock.

Men will have to clear away the ruins and rebuild the world, and everybody will have to pay—have already paid—the innocent and the red-handed.

One cannot smash up the furniture in a night of madness and wake up to an orderly house.

Three hundred years ago John Donne said "No man is an island, entire of itself. . . . every man is involved in mankind." it is a lesson the world will have to learn—that the fury of a little paper-hanger in Austria means that a young cowboy in Arizona, who never heard of him, will have to die.

If the world has learned that all nations are involved in each other, it can be the beginning of a golden age, gadgets or no gadgets.

—August 19, 1944

Enchantment

The fair is a place of superlatives—the biggest pumpkins, the wildest steers, the yellowest corn, the tenderest cake, the clearest jelly, the tallest grass. Everything is the biggest and the best.

It is a place for the credulous, and the scoffingest person begins to get star-eyed if he stays around a while.

When a fellow has just seen a 950-pound hog, it is easy to believe that just inside that tent is a woman eleven feet around the middle. After he has

48

feasted his eye upon the most enticing apples, who can blame him if he is drawn into a show on the promise of seeing the world's most daring beauties? Where there are apples, there must be Eves.

And if he comes home with a potato peeler that no one can work, don't say a word. Didn't he see the miracle of plastics made into everything from zippers to the dome in a bomber?

The fair is a place where people become children for a few hours. The whirling, spinning, roaring mass of lights and colors and sounds is surely the land of enchantment. And if some of the magic makers are a trifle tough and hard of countenance, one barely notices it.

Everything is the best, the only, the fairest, the bravest. The gaudy and shabby and cheap are saved from scorn by their lack of pretense.

But there is one realist on the fairgrounds. In the very midst of the milling mass, a placard on a stand bears these brief, terse words, "Aspirin, 2 for 5 cents."

And there is eating. Pink floss candy is typical—airy spun stuff that is nothing but froth, yet leaves a lingering sweetness. "Snowballs," pop, ice cream, peanuts, popcorn, hot dogs, and all the old favorites.

It there a saint who watches over digestion at fair time?

—September 13, 1944

Speech of a Candidate Who Has Been Inoculated With Truth Serum

Well, folks, here we are up against another election, and I am one of the candidates.

I didn't much want to run, but it seemed a good time to get a toehold in the Statehouse. Things may get tougher after the war, and I haven't been very successful in my own business.

I don't like hard work anymore and I'm not young. So I thought I'd see what I could do in politics.

There's no use to beat about the bush in this matter of taxes. They're high, and as long as we keep running to the Government for a lot of fancy knick-knacks, they're going to be high.

After the war you'll want a lot of new lakes and parks and overpasses and city halls, and I guess you can get them. But remember, they cost money. Don't squeal when it comes time to pay.

You can't fix up your own house, buy a car and take a trip without its costing you. Neither can the Government, and the Government is you.

I'd like to help the farmer, but I'm no magician. I can't make it rain or stop raining, shine or stop shining. I can't control the grasshopper, the cinch bug, or the Hessian fly. I can't even control my own family.

And that is one of the reasons I want to be elected.

My wife has a brother and I have a cousin or two who can't seem to hold onto any kind of a job, and if I'm elected I'm going to try to get them on the payroll. It's either that or help support them myself.

other reverses. Like a root growing in the earth, he did not stop when he hit a rock—he turned aside and started again.

He would have made a great pioneer, had circumstances set his feet on the covered wagon trail, the kind of man who pushed on when the post office caught up with him.

But he was destined to lead men thru the tall grasses of new ideas and into the forests of fresh experiments.

How greatly the world has been diminished by his untimely passing can never be known. History does not play a repeat performance with a new ending. It happens and that is the way it has to be.

But the Arab, the Turk, the Italian, the Chinese, the South American—it may be that the lives of all people everywhere will be different in some way because Franklin Roosevelt did not live to finish his work.

His death will lift the common will to higher resolve and greater courage. The years of the war have seen former issues fade in the light of the great hope for a world of peace, and in that hope the nation looked to their President.

Let there be no sighing that his last years were spent in bearing heavy burdens, spent in pain and weariness over problems that racked the soul. It was the way such a man would want it to be.

His was not a quiet spirit, and the tired body endured until it was released for the long sleep.

—April 16, 1945

Two Men

In a drawer of my desk I found a newspaper dated January 30, 1933. In the middle of the front page was a two-column picture labeled, "Adolf Hitler, who today achieved his ambition to become chancellor of Germany."

The crumbling old paper chanced to be lying near an edition of the same publication for May 1, 1945. In almost the same position on page one was another two-column cut of the same man, under the big head, "Hitler Killed in Berlin."

Sharing the front page with Hitler in the 1933 paper was President-Elect Franklin D. Roosevelt. The stories are startlingly similar. The Hitler Cabinet was named. Speculations were made about the Roosevelt Cabinet.

These two men came to the heads of their countries at about the same time. Both achieved tremendous power and attracted masses. Both were admired, even fanatically adored. Both held their power largely thru their personalities. Both died within the last month.

But there the likeness stops. Hitler used his power for violence, which was to destroy himself and his country and plunge the world into blood. Roosevelt hoped to bring security to the common man.

After a few farce sessions of enforced "ya" voting, Hitler dissolved the Reichstag, due to an "emergency."

But because Roosevelt lived in a "decadent democracy," he had to hold his power thru free, regular elections. He had many bouts with Congress. Some he won, some he lost. But the Congress, chosen in a free election by the people, continued to meet.

Roosevelt had enemies who criticized him, who denounced him bitterly in press, radio, and public speech. No critic was silenced or could have been silenced by his edict. Hitler's enemies were "liquidated" or sent to concentration camps.

When Roosevelt died, the world grieved. Even his enemies respected him and admired his spirit. When Hitler died, the world rejoiced. The only regret was that dying was too good.

Two men whose lives are strangely parallel, but who were worlds apart.

—May 5, 1945

Remember When?

Dwight Eisenhower won the surrender of the German armies—and returned to win his own country. Wherever he has gone, people have been genuinely moved by his sincerity and friendliness.

Perhaps Abilene has done a service to the world in setting a new kind of welcome for a conquering general.

Warriors have come proudly home with kings chained to their chariot wheels, and followed by hundreds of beautiful maidens, brought home as prizes. They have returned with loot and slaves to receive acclaim. The occasions have been tributes to the might of the conqueror.

But last Friday a great general came home to a small town. He brought no captives or rich plunder. He came to see his family and his old home.

The day was not a military celebration. It was a gentle looking back, from days of a man's childhood, thru the years he was a boy and a young man.

It was a kind of "Remember when" day—the good, mellow, nostalgic talk that is talked by old friends who have been long apart.

General Eisenhower has said he wants only to return to his home, as the other soldiers will do. He has guided our armies to victory in the first part of the war. It may be that he can do great a service in leading the way back to peaceful living.

—June 25, 1945

As Handsome Does

She was plain, stout, and middle-aged. Her hair was thin and graying. Nobody gave her a second look as she got on the train, nobody but a young soldier, private first class.

He gave her his seat—and was the luckiest fellow on the train.

At the next stop the place beside the woman was vacated, and the soldier sat down with her.

Porters came thru the coach at noon offering dry butterless sandwiches. Then it was that the woman opened a box and took from it food that made every passenger within sight start drooling.

Chicken fried to a golden crisp, pickles, olives, rich chocolate cake, fresh tomatoes, a big box of nuts—she spread it out and invited the soldier to eat with her. She pressed generous helpings upon him and bought coffee for both of them.

In the evening she insisted on taking him to the diner and buying him a meal.

The next noon another box was opened yielding sandwiches of thick fried ham, fruit, doughnuts, celery crisp in oiled paper. And again she bought coffee.

For two days, between Oregon and Colorado, she fed the soldier, played cards with him, shared magazines.

"She said right out that she was fifty-four and laughed about it," the woman who told me reported. "She was large and not nice-looking, but she sure knew how to fix a lunch."

(Note to traveling soldiers: Tho it may sound like a fairy-book tale, this is a true story. This column does not, however, guarantee that all plain, stout, gray, middle-aged women come equipped with luscious lunches and generous impulses.

You will be nice to such at your own risk. We can not assume any responsibility.)

—July 20, 1945

To Live Forever

Once a little girl, when she began to sense the mysteries of the universe, turned to her mother and cried, "I want to live forever—I've just got to see how the world turns out!"

A person feels that way as the power of the atomic bomb is realized and the world begins to dream of what it could mean.

Nearly every person believes in ultimate, miraculous good. It is more than hope. It is a law of growth. It is a vital, simple belief in mankind, a tribute to some spark within him.

And the long hill that man has trudged justifies the faith that he will do big things. He raised up on two feet and slowly learned to use the great forces of the earth — fire, metal, gunpowder, printing, steam, electricity—learned in a hard school where he made his own speech and tools and text—worked his way through, too, didn't have a cent.

Dorothy Thompson says the atomic bomb puts the whole war into the background. Man has discovered the original source of all energy, the source that causes the sun eternally to burn, the source of inexhaustible wealth."

The new bomb is too horrible to be used in future wars. There is no defense against it—"Man is not made to fight atomic energy or to go to war against the sun." There must be control by a world state.

Perhaps this is an hour equal to the one when man first felt the power of a stone ax in his hand, or gazed at the first fire he had made, or when the first words trembled over a wire.

Perhaps it is an hour to mark the history books, and you find you are more excited than surprised.

For you have always known in your heart, with a shy faith, that great things would come. You have always believed in miracles. You don't like to brag, since man is a distant cousin on your father's side, but you have always known he was going to amount to something.

And it makes you, like the little girl, want to live forever.

—August 13, 1945

The Spirit and a Stone Doorstep

I went back home and found the old house in which I was born filled with dull coppery oats piled against green wallpaper. The windows were boarded, the doors nailed shut.

In one corner stands the old organ my mother saved turkey money to buy—a six octave Beckwith Grand from Sears-Roebuck. It is as intricately ornate as a cathedral and has as many pockets as a pair of overalls.

I looked at my face in the mirror and smiled to think it had once reflected that same face freckled and pigtailed.

One of the four big mulberry trees had been cut down. Others were dying at the top. Except for the sure knowledge that trees and house and well had not been moved, I could not have believed the vast rolling spaces I remembered could have shrunk so small.

The only things untouched were the stone doorsteps, the big limestone rocks worn smooth from years of footsteps, bare feet and shod feet, wind and weather and scrubbing. Men and women and children sitting on them summer evenings, babies climbing over them — all who passed the threshold smoothed and polished the hard stone, but a hundred generations could not wear it down.

I searched my mind for the truth...The little girl seemed someone I had known and loved. I would recall that she said this or that—a very dear little girl truly, but she must be a grown woman by now. There was tenderness but not pain in remembering her.

The old home place has been emotionalized. People travel back to see it and their hearts are heavy.

They think they are grieving for a house trembling with years, for dying

55

trees and old forgotten things, but their tears are for their lost youth, for the changes that have come to them.

That childhood should seem so lost and sad is a mark against adult living. Other periods of years should be as precious, but they are darkened by the clouds of failure and remorse.

Perhaps we bungle our lives until the tormented mind takes refuge in the innocence of young years. Contentment sprang so easy from the rich early soil that we will not work to make it grow on the worn fields of later years. It is a too easy giving up. We flee to the security of the past rather than try to learn a new kind of happiness.

Childhood is simple and free. The spirit can grow boundlessly, but in older years it is warped and scarred trying to fit into rules and measures.

A man looks back to escape the future. The goodness of childhood is gone, but he knows that is the answer to his wanting—to be simple and free again, to be as a child.

So the place of his childhood becomes a symbol. He sets his feet on the rich green ground of memory and his heart is broken when he finds decay.

But it is the decay of his own spirit he unknowingly grieves, and that is the one thing that can be impervious to time. Wood and tree and fence decay.

But a man's spirit can outlast a stone doorstep.

—September 15, 1945

* * *

In speaking of marriage to a daughter, a woman manages to intimate that it is a great misfortune, and at the same time convey the impression that it is a misfortune that must not be missed.

One of the sad things of life is the difficulty of checking up on your face cream.

You my feel that it is not doing you much good, but on the other hand, you can never be sure what you would have looked like without it.

—September 29, 1945

* * *

Peace came so suddenly it found those steady long-range planners, the greeting card makers, unprepared.

Hardly had the first bombs been dropped than cards were in the racks to carry best wishes to a Dear Cousin in the Marines, to a Nice Nephew in Navy Blue, or to Uncle's Stepson in the Coast Guard. No kin was forgotten.

But the other day a girl was looking for a card to tell a friend she was glad he was a civillian (meaning she was glad he was in circulation again), and she could find nothing tailored for the occasion.

—October 4, 1945

City Girl

A number of years ago the son of a good solid family went to Chicago to try himself out on the world.

A few months later he beamed himself home with a strange young thing, who, he proudly told his parents, was going to marry him, and wasn't he lucky?

The parents didn't think so, but they kept it to themselves.

The girl wore little red shoes with heels four inches high, in a day when red shoes were not worn in their town by girls over six years old. Her hair was a bright cloud around her face, she ran in and out of the house like she had known them always—an empty-headed little fluff who laughed at everything.

They looked at each other miserably and asked how he could do that to them, their boy they had brought up so carefully.

That was fifteen years ago.

She still laughs at everything. She still fluffs out her hair. She still runs in and out the house. She still wears red shoes.

And all of these traits were stout family assets, her father-in-law declares, better than money in the bank.

There were times when there wasn't much money in the bank, when there was sickness and trouble and discouragement. But the girl's bright laughing little ways held firm.

Her mother-in-law has never known a better mother than the girl turned out to be—she brought up the most beautiful, the most perfect grandchildren that ever were.

They're a little sheepish about it now, but they remember.

If they had had their way, they would have married their boy to the quiet studious little girl down the street. They figured she'd make him a good, steady wife.

—October 21, 1945

* * *

A farm woman laid a curving stone path from the kitchen door to the well. She thought it was prettier that way and she wanted more prettiness.

Her husband threw a board across the neck of the curve and walks to the well and back in a straight line.

She carries the water around the curve and does not mind the extra steps.

She thinks it is prettier that way.

—November 1, 1945

* * *

A woman finds comfort in this rule: As long as you hurt in only one leg, it's not old age, for one leg is as old as the other.

It's just rheumatism.

—November 6, 1945

57

Not My Fault

Most of the people in the world, I expect, feel they have lived good lives if they can point to the calamities all about them and say, "I didn't do it. It's not my fault."

But that is not enough. When something goes wrong, it does not matter much whose fault it was. The suffering and loss are the same.

Which driver was to blame is not important if both are killed in the accident.

Whether the fire started from baby's matches, mamma's cigarette, or Junior's chemistry set is of little consequence when the house is in ashes. All are equally homeless.

And when the love of two people has turned to bitterness, both are the losers, however it came about. Accusations are of no moment.

No matter who started the trouble, the fire, the quarrel, the fight, all who are concerned suffer the consequences.

The rest of the world blames Germany and Japan for the war. We say virtuously that we did not fight till attacked—but our own men died the same as the Germans and Japanese.

There will not be peace in the world until nations are more eager to prevent war than to place blame. Wars, like cyclones and rattlesnakes, give a little warning before they strike, and that is the time to fight a war.

Disaster is too costly for any smug assertions of innocence or any pointing of fingers. Trying war criminals does not bring the dead back to life.

The whole history of human trouble is that it is easier to destroy than to create. Nations have found it easier to stir up the people, arm them, and fight, then to stop a war before it begins.

We will be getting along toward the millennium when our desire to clear ourself of blame is replaced by a feeling of guilt if we have not tried to prevent a disaster.

Man is bound to man. If we do not help each other so that all may escape, we will perish together. No matter whose fault it is.

—December 7, 1945

*   *   *

I've noticed that the people who brag most about a great-great-grandfather who was in the revolution are the kind of people who would never start a revolution themselves.

—January 4, 1946

*   *   *

I wonder if preachers don't get tired of being pushed off with women all the time, and having men apologize if they forget and use a rough word in their hearing.

A woman wrote to a guest she had invited to a meeting, "There won't be any men present except of course the preacher."

It's enough to make a person start chewing tobacco.

—January 4, 1946

*   *   *

Even the shapely plaster leg at one of the hosiery counters has lost its last stocking:

"We hated to," sighed a woman who would sell them if they had any, "but somebody wanted to buy it and we had to take it off."

The leg still dangles a pair of ruffled garters.

And, oh yes, if you want an empty box to ship anything away in, there are plenty in the stocking departments. They look better than empty shelves.

Stockings give store managers chills and shudders. Every time the paper says anything about nylons being released or being made or soon to be plentiful—or even that a pair of nylons was bought one day in an Oklahoma store—a wave sweeps over them.

It's as hot as handling stolen rubies.

—January 5, 1946

*   *   *

When you look ahead to something for a long time and want it very much, you keep thinking how it might happen, how it will be. And when it comes, it has its own way.

One of these is how it will be when your boy comes home.

I had pictured it many times—the house would be fresh and clean and his room all ready for him, a fire would be blazing in the fireplace, good things would be in the refrigerator, and I would be wearing a pretty dress.

He came, early in the morning the day before Christmas, and it was not as I had planned it at all.

Then I knew it was something beyond plans, that however it happened, it would be right.

The door opened and he was in the house, running up the stairs, just as he used to do, and in a little while it was as tho he had never been away.

—January 6, 1946

*   *   *

Belief in magic is still in the world. I saw it on the face of a little girl in the post office.

"Push the letter thru that hole and daddy will get it," her mother said.

The child, her face elfin under a flared wool bonnet, held the letter a delicious second, then let it slide away.

The smile she turned upward was a light fueled by wonder and faith.

The post office had better see that that letter is delivered.

—January 10, 1946

59

* * *

Who would have thought along in the middle thirties that in ten years little curly-haired Shirley Temple would be playing in a movie which mothers would sigh that they wished their daughters who are Shirley's age "didn't have to see?"

—January 16, 1946

Cowhand

Sure, he'd been a cowhand. He'd rounded up cattle at Price, in Northwest Texas, thirty-some years ago, on the Mule Shoe Ranch.

He was seventeen and had had a little trouble at home. He'd show them he could make his own living. And there he was in Price showing them.

But disillusion yourself about cattleherding. It wasn't like the movies.

And disillusion yourself about Price. It wasn't any romantic frontier town with Saturday-night dances and street shootings and pretty school teachers.

It was nothing but a boxcar set down in the sand. No post office. They didn't need a post office. Nobody got any mail.

A cattleman from the Flint Hills of Kansas described the grass as a quarter of an inch high and a quarter of a mile apart. How the cattle lived on the mesquite and cactus and prickly pear he never knew, but they did live.

The cowhands were fed from a chuck wagon, which does not mean it was chuckfull of good things to eat.

Coffee and beans and sourdough was the fare. He never did know how sourdough bread tasted; they had to eat it burning hot because they couldn't stand to smell it when it cooled.

They didn't have any baggage only their blanket and they didn't do any washing. All they wore was a shirt and Levis; they kept them on till they wore out, then threw them away and got more.

Maybe they didn't stay very fresh, but there was plenty of room to keep a distance from each other.

Sometimes they played a little poker around the campfire or a lantern light, but soon after dark they rolled up in their blankets and went to sleep.

Yes, sure it was out under the stars—and under the wind and under the rain and it wasn't romantic. They got to sleep quick to forget the hard ground, and about that time the cook was beating on a tin pan and they had to get up and saddle the horses and push down more beans and coffee and sourdough.

No guitar twanging, no singing about being buried out on the prairie. Just ride from sunup to dark and get up and ride again the next day.

I said it must have been a hard life—seventeen and away from home. Poor kid.

"Poor kid!" He was silent a long minute. "It was the best time in my life and I wish I was there again."

—January 22, 1946

Permanent

The longest-suffering man of the week was the farmer who took his wife to town to have a permanent.

He left her at the beauty shop and went ahead marketing the cream and buying feed. He got the groceries and took shoes to be half-soled.

Back at the beauty shop to inquire and told that his wife had just "gone under the drier for the first time."

Which set him to wondering if it was something like drowning.

He went back to the grocery store meaning to sit and talk, but found women in the the chairs aound the stove. What was the country coming to when women sat around the grocery stove swapping stories?

Driven to the barber shop, he was forced to have his hair clipped, tho he didn't want to. He relaxed and talked to the boys about cattle and crop prospects and strikes and politics.

At the beauty shop the attendant smiled at him like a nurse in the delivery room and said, "Another fifteen minutes."

He went to the filling station and had gas put in the car, tires and battery checked, and the antifreeze tested.

Another trip to the beauty shop and another promise of delivery in fifteen minutes.

He walked around town and looked at the houses and thought what he would do to each one if it was his.

Then, just as the western hills cut a slice off the setting sun, his wife was handed to him, her face drawn and her hair likewise.

They got into the car and drove away.

"I'll never have another one," she said, her voice tight and strained. Tears stood in her eyes as she looked at her frizzed top in the windshield mirror.

That was what she always said after a permanent.

"Now, mommy, don't fret," he said gently. You know it will straighten out.

—January 24, 1946

*   *   *

In their business matters the ladies' clubs do not ever buy or pay or sell. They purchase and reimburse and dispose of.

—January 27, 1946

Dry Day

A sheaf of questions and answers came from the Air Press Service, with the suggestion that some of it might be used "on a dry day." A dry day in this business is the same as the rainy day people are always being adjured to save for.

A dry day, huh?

Of course I could have puffed up and sputtered that it would be a dry day indeed. But a dozen years of columning, with their attendant dry days, condition a person to some humility.

—February 8, 1946

*   *   *

When the grocer dumps a box of apples into the bin for customers to pick over, evolution goes into reverse. It is the unfittest that survive.

—March 7, 1946

Flint Hills

After four years we went back to the Flint Hills and found the Chase County people had taken good care of them.

A number of houses and roads and bridges, and even a few people, were a little changed, but the Flint Hills lifted the same long, clean lines to the sky.

As you leave the valley, the little creeks and draws are fringed with trees, but on the upland they fall back and give way to long rounded slopes and ridges as calm as time.

They are soft peach and pale violet and taupe and beige and tan and rust. Under the warm gold of the sun they look like a monstrous sand heap a giant's child might play in.

Stand among the hills and give yourself to forgetfulness: conflicts and frustrations fall away as tiredness when a weary man sinks into his bed at night.

The Flint Hills would be the place for a permanent home for the United Nations Organization.

A delegate might glimpse a vision of world peace if he could arise every morning to a clean bare sweep of hills all around him up to the edge of the sky.

He could forget the intrigues of bristling embassies as he watched the topaz turn to emerald in spring; and the plunder and propaganda of world capitals would seem far beyond a horizon where turquoise and purple faded into a blue sky.

In the peace of the Flint Hills the peace of the world would not seem impossible, but it is more likely the delegate would forget the world entirely.

But do not start any movements, please. It would not be well to clutter up the hills with sound and tumult and noisy comings and goings.

The Flint Hills are simple and quiet and timeless. They belong to the

62

people who live there, to men who ride in seasoned boots and weathered hats, to men who farm the little valleys and pasture the big hills, to women who look out their kitchen window every day at a familiar curve of sky.

And to any soul attuned to beauty and peace.

—March 8, 1946

* * *

The person who applies logic to all his actions is necessarily pretty well satisfied with himself. He has fitted himself into the pattern that seems most desirable to him.

Consequently he is poorly equipped to understand the man in whose life logic is not a ruling force.

Logic is like Esperanto. It would work all right if everybody used it. So would French or Chinese or English.

—March 23, 1946

* * *

Gromyko joins Al Smith and Garbo as one who is going to take a walk and thinks he will go home.

—March 30, 1946

Wildflowers in Her Hair

A woman said a surprising thing.

It began with the simple remark that when she went away for her vacation, she always wore wildflowers in her hair. She added, "I'm an entirely different person when I'm away."

Her husband is in a public job and travels all during the summer. It is then that she takes the children and goes to the ocean or the mountains.

"It's simply wonderful," she said, "to go away some place where you are not known and be yourself."

When she is away she seems to fall in naturally with gay, spirited people, and she is pleased that they seem to like her.

She enjoys smoking on her vacation. When she is at home she does not smoke. Some people who are in authority would not approve.

Once out of town she takes on a new personality as well as new clothes. She wears play suits, shorts, sandals, bright and gay and easy things that would make her feel conspicuous at home.

The days are easy and free. She plays with the children—no obligations, no "position" to fill, nothing to live up to.

But when the summer is ended—

She can't bear to think of coming back to the old life, she can't bear to answer the telephone, to make plans for organizations, and start going to things.

Her friends exclaim how different she looks.

63

"I am different," she says. "When I'm away I'm the kind of a person I want to be. It's the kind of a person I'd like to be all the time."

Then why not be?

But I knew the answer. I knew the little grooves of what people are supposed to do and be, all the unwritten, stiff, stifling forms of activity thought suitable for a respectable cultured woman who has a "place" in the community to maintain.

The strange thing is that perhaps half the women she knows are restless in the little grooves.

Many women would like to be themselves in a freer, simpler way of living, but they are afraid to let go of the kind of life that is "accepted." They are afraid of being lonely and shut out.

"I wonder why you have to go clear away to do a better job of being yourself," the woman said. The "wonderful feeling" lasts quite a while, but by spring not a speck of it is left.

"Right now," she said, "I'm as grim as death."

—May 19, 1946

The Hardships of Life

The wisdom of children is to be trusted. Their observation is fresh, their thinking uncluttered.

So I said to Dorothy Anne, "What shall I write about fathers for Father's Day?"

She thought for only a moment before answering, "They stand the hardships of life."

The reply was a bit startling. I didn't suppose the average nine-year-old child knew anything about the hardships of life.

"What hardships?" I asked.

"Oh, you know, when something gets the matter with the car, it's always the father that gets out and fixes it."

I understood. If there is one time I concede that man is the rightful master of the earth, it is when something is the matter with the car.

Nor should I have been surprised that a child, especially a female child in a family whose car is never of the latest vintage, should think of the management of a car as one of the major hardships of life.

"What other hardships do fathers have?" I pursued.

"They make the money," she said simply.

There it was: A father fixed the car and made the money, certainly both major responsibilities.

Women and children spend most of the money. They have the pleasure of selecting and choosing; they plan social affairs and vacations.

Father is too busy making the money.

But when trouble or sorrow strikes, then it is his turn to act, for his are the last-ditch responsibilities.

He is the one who sees the doctor, the lawyer, the sheriff, the banker, the undertaker. He is the one who goes when there is a knock at the door in the dead of night. He stands between his family and trouble, sparing them what pain and shock and discomfort he can take upon himself.

When Jesus wanted a symbol of the love of God for humanity, he chose the love of a father for his children, not a mother, whose love is often blind and possessive and unreasoning, but a father, whose love is tender and compassionate, watchful and protecting.

—June 9, 1946

* * *

I do not look ahead to television with any great eagerness, but if it will stop radio actresses from indicating emotion by panting, it will be worth while.

When a stage or screen actress receives a staggering blow, she can go limp, she can sink into a chair, she can stare straight ahead, she can set her face in drooping lines, any of which can fill a silence and get over the idea that the poor thing is suffering.

But on the radio there is nothing but silence.

So she pants, or gasps, and sounds so much like a dog on a hot day that the delicate illusion is lost.

—June 20, 1946

Editor

An editor is a peculiarly bedeviled man, always skirting the dangers of losing his own soul or being horsewhipped.

If his paper does not please people, they will not take it; if he makes pleasing them his aim, they will scorn and disdain him.

He has many decisions to make and not much time to make them.

He must be able to decide when to leave a name out of the paper for the sake of kindness; he must know when he leaves it out whether it is from kindness or weakness; and he must know when he prints it whether it is from pique or principle.

He must have the sensitiveness to appreciate a child's naivete, and the worldliness to deal with the big boys.

He must know how to decline spring poetry without stopping the spring.

His hardest job will be resisting the big ideas that members of his own profession pull out of silk hats, rosy bait for propaganda.

He must beware of suggestions from good advertisers.

He must be alert to consider the ideas of others, but firm in his own decisions.

He has to know whether those decisions are based on fact or fear or appeasement or personal issues. Others will have their opinions about it; he must know for dead sure.

He must not brood. If he cannot wipe the slate clean and say, "Next week is another week; tomorrow is another day," he will flounder and be lost.

And above all, an editor must be big enough to be humble, for when the paper comes out he will need humility more than any of the graces.

—August 2, 1946

* * *

A new use has been found for the manure spreader, which stands idle much of the time.

Two different aspirants to public office have plastered their posters on one such machine standing near the highway.

—September 27, 1946

Impudent Brightness

The eye-lingeringest hat in this region is Renna Hunter's Lily Dache model brought home from New York.

It's a straight-setting hat, narrow in stern, wider at the bow, with a lot of red plaid taffeta wadded over the top deck and a big full fuchsia rose pointing due front along the starboard bulkhead.

Renna wore it at a club meeting with a smooth gray dress, and I bet every woman there was aching to try it on.

But nobody could, because town women keep their hats on at afternoon meetings, an annoying style. In the country or a little town it would be an offense to the hostess not to take off your hat and lay it on the bed.

What enticement in a bedful of hats! It takes a strong will to resist them. You slip upstairs a little late, to leave your own, and there they are, like a coopful of chickens into which a few pheasants and parrots and love birds have strayed.

The hum of talk from down below stops suddenly and you know the meeting is beginning. You ought to hurry right down so as not to miss a word of the secretary's report, but you stand a breathless moment, and fly to the mirror with the brightest and gayest to see how it looks on you.

About this Lily Dache hat—there's nothing to hat designing but a little nerve. The Dache hat takes your eye because Lily threw off her inhibitions and let herself go.

In one sense there is little difference between the hats worn by the very stylish and those who never saw a fashion book in their lives—both are made by women who have the courage to indulge a love of color.

Peasant women and others who are unshackled by style clap gay, reckless headdresses on themselves, whatever they find pleasing, and wear them with innocent charm.

Famous designers do the same thing, and women who want to be different wear the pert models insouciantly.

66

At both ends of fashion is impudent brightness, while in between on the misty flat streets and dusty roads, women are topped with the timid, inoffensive headgear that will "go with everything."

—October 25, 1946

Waste

Women spend sixty-six and two-thirds percent of their time looking out for their clothes.

They must be careful not to walk in weeds or tall grass. They'd snag their stockings. Anyway, they couldn't walk far or they would ruin their shoes.

Veils and flowers and feathers are to be held on to in a wind, and delicate lapel pins must be guarded.

A woman can not put on her clothes and forget about them. She has to keep her dress pulled down and her stockings pulled up. Seams have to be straightened, blouses tucked in, the skirt placket pulled around to the side, and there must be pauses to renew makeup and comb hair.

She has to hold on to her hat and her purse, and watch about her gloves and handkerchief.

The amazing thing is that she can do all that she does and still keep herself tucked in and smoothed down. If all a woman's energy is ever released for positive doing, she will rule the world—and I don't want anybody writing in to say that she does rule it.

—November 6, 1946

Enchanted Forest

It was my unreliable sense of direction that led me into the enchanted forest.

I had come out of the grocery and was looking around the parking lot for my car. I was sure I had left it in a certain row, but I walked behind all the cars and looked carefully at the tags and it was not there.

Cars backed out and drove in all around me. Drivers gave me cool or amused or hard looks. I stood still, trying to remember where I had stopped.

From behind me came the sound of a high little voice, as clear as water trickling thru grass.

"What are you looking for, woman?" it asked.

Warmed that someone was interested in my distress, I turned and looked straight into another world. A well-worn car, but not so worn or battered as the 1936 Chevie I was searching for, was filled with tiny children. There were six, looking like six lovely pale flowers.

The girl who had spoken to me stood in the back part of the car and smiled faintly. Her eyes were bright brown velvet and her skin was pale

67

white silk. She was slim and tiny, and her face was pointed like a heart.

Beside her stood a smaller girl, her brown eyes grayer brown, her small face rounder. A third girl smiled over the heads of the two.

In the front end were two wee boys. One said,"I'm the only one of us that goes to school." His slim little face was bright and joyous. Sitting on the seat was a boy about two with the wistfulest little face I have ever seen. His eyes very, very dark and very round, and his face was as delicate and white as fine china.

The children stood quietly, almost too quietly. They smiled gently and when they spoke it was about something that included all of them. They were neither polite nor impolite. They were interested and curious and friendly and unafraid yet shy and modest.

Around us surged tired-faced people with sacks of groceries, people from stores and offices and shops, stout and thin and tall and short people, moving in and out.

The six little elves in the car were from another world. Now I knew I was lost. I was not in a parking lot hunting for a car. I had wandered into an enchanted forest peopled by lovely little white fairies and elves, eager little wistful creatures who peeped curiously into my grocery sack.

—January 28, 1947

* * *

Much as I would like to improve my appearance, I cannot risk using the soap recommended by a well-known movie star in a new magazine. She has lost three husbands, one right after the other. Maybe she can afford it, but I don't have three husbands to lose.

—February 16, 1947

Who's World

Women, said Doris Fleeson in a luncheon address, have reached their lowest point in years in the matter of holding important jobs of wielding influence in national affairs. No women are in the Cabinet or Senate, or important diplomatic posts, and only five are in the House of Representatives.

One reason that not many women hold office is because they approach politics as a kind of Ladies' Aid or auxiliary. Women are the auxiliary organizers. They band together for no better reason than because their men do the same kind of work.

They have not expected any great reward from politics nor prepared themselves to qualify for it. To sit on platforms, to wear corsages, to make the responses, and to have "one woman on the board" has been enough for the majority.

Women have the intelligence, they have the public interest, but they do not have the drive and push that it takes to win a big office, in the way offices have been won in the past. If they want to sit in high places they will have to play politics as avidly as they do bridge.

Women have a great untouched political strength. It is that there are lots of them. Enough to change the ways of politics and the ways of getting offices. If they would educate themselves as leaders, and unite in one purpose, they could elect each other to all the offices, and change the course of the world. It is their world as much as it is men's.

But it won't happen in '48.

—May 21, 1947

The Attitude

I believe it was William James who said, "Assume the attitude and the feeling will follow." I never quite accepted it, but when I was mending a coat a few days ago I knew what he meant.

It was an old coat which had not grown with the child. Body and sleeves had to be let down, the lining mended in a dozen places, the fabric of the coat darned, buttons sewed on.

It was a grubby, hateful job. I went at it stiff and uncompromising, resentful of the time it was using up.

But as I worked something began to happen. My annoyance was slowly dissolved and the needle flickered from negative into positive.

First I lost my active distaste for the job, and then I began to feel pleasure in giving new life to the old garment, a thin little pleasure that crept over me like electricity flowing into a stove turned to the lowest unit.

But presently there was a faint glow and the mending changed from a dull bout with time to a job in which I was interested, tho I am not pretending that I would not rather have cut something out of exciting new material to sew.

William James may never have mended a coat, but he knew something about the human mind.

—May 23, 1947

Hunger

"Straighten your tie, dad," a boy was always saying to his father.

The man would give it a little pull to center, and answer, "When you get my age, you won't think about your tie, either."

It is useless to say to the young, grieving over a slight or a failure, that it does not matter. You know it will pass and not be remembered, but the moment is raw and bleeding.

When you are sore from hurt or defeat, you wouldn't like to be told it doesn't matter.

It does not matter whether I eat my supper tonight on linen or on oilcloth, if I have enough to eat. Nor what my coat is made of, if it keeps me warm. It makes no difference whether my car is old or new, so it runs. Nor whether I live in two rooms or ten, if the roof does not leak.

These things are not important.

What is important? What is the big thing? What does matter, in the end?

What mattered to the people lying under the flowers in the graveyards today? Ask them. Shout at them. Make them answer.

There is a line from Robinson Jeffers: "Life with no more desire than a stone."

Life is a length of days burning out like a fire. It begins with no desire but food, and flames brightly until every desire is consumed but the first.

But the flame is never fed. It licks out after each twig and stick, and its hunger is never satisfied.

Life is a man hunting in the dark for something he has never seen.

It must be somewhere. It must be something he has never seen.

It must be somewhere. It must be something. Where is it? What is it?

What would quiet the heart's loneliness? What would ease the spirit's pain? What is it we spend our lives looking for?

A stone? But life is eager and searching. The heart is hungry for food it never finds.

Ask the people in the graves. Ask if they found it.

—May 30, 1947

Ma, They're Laughing at Me

Soon as vacations get under way, travelers will start writing back home to the newspapers whining that people are making fun of Kansas.

The first principle of joking is to find a receiver who takes himself quite seriously. Any traveling Kansan so humorless as to be upset by a little kidding had better stay at home and read the KIDC literature.

Kidding visitors from another section is the favorite pastime of the nation. When a radio comedian wants to get a real deep hard laugh, he says "I'm from Brooklyn." It is always very funny.

Who has not heard Kansans poking fun at visitors from Texas or Missouri or Tennessee or Arkansas or New England or California? And the visitors, if they are bright, return a few sharp thrusts.

It is a regional game of wits. One needs to know some answers.

Mrs. Frank Boyd did. When she was a girl and was Mame Alexander, one of a large family where every member worked, she went in to Garnett to go to high school.

One of Mame's jobs on the farm was to drive a team of mules. The town children learned of it and began calling her Alexander the Mule Driver.

Mame did not run home and tell the family that the town kids were

70

making fun of her. She did not cry and say she would never go to that school again.

The dearest wish and hope of her life was to go to school and nothing could spoil it. She laughed the loudest and quickest of any at the mule driver joke.

She talked about mule driving and made it seem so exciting that every little stinker in the mob began envying the girl who was smart enough and brave enough to drive a pair of big, stubborn mules.

When a person is disturbed by criticism it is because there are some doubts in his mind.

Mame Alexander had no doubts about the worthiness and good repute of mule driving. She was not embarrassed or apologetic. She knew the value of a team of mules and of the work they did.

Run along to the mountains and the seashore and don't forget to pack, along with your change of clothes, a sense of the fitness of things.

—June 6, 1947

Competition

The bus was crowded, but I found a seat in the back across from a small, slight soldier who was sitting with a plump blonde in slacks.

It was easy to see he was not a boy new in uniform. His face had that alert, shifting, wary look of a man who likes excitement, plus the usual scar.

He was a jockey, two weeks out of Korea, and going home with his discharge to Lexington, Ky., and the blue grass—going home with 34 pounds more than he took away, a calamity in the life of a jockey.

He would have to stop riding, but he would never live away from horses. Now he would train them for other men to ride.

I wanted to hear about jockeying, but the blonde favored conversation in low monosyllables—not about horses, I was certain.

The blonde and I were pretty evenly matched. She had me on pounds, but I had her on years. She wore bright lipstick that showed off well as her mouth flashed open and shut over her gum, I wore lipstick too.

She worked on him with sideways glances. I drew him out with questions.

I wanted him to talk about himself. She wanted him to talk about her. That gave me an edge there. For what man can resist telling the story of his life with someone leaning across a narrow bus aisle to catch every word?

How did it feel to sit on a horse with your feet drawn up, tearing down the track like wind, hearing the enemy behind you?

"Oh, it just gets to be a business," he shrugged, but I knew he did not mean it.

Horses? You have to learn each one. "You handle 'em the way you do a woman," he said with his best man-of-the-world look. "Some you coax with pretty words. Some you treat rough."

The blonde's pretty red mouth was in a pout. She gave us a sullen look and began talking to him. He reached over and patted her mane.

I settled back. The next inning was hers.

—June 8, 1947

Moreish

A couple of Kansans stopped at Harrison, Ark., during the strawberry festival.

The waitress at the little restaurant where they went for supper started off with the statement that their strawberry shortcake was the best strawberry shortcake in Arkansas and that meant in the world.

"Bring me a dish of it," one of the men said.

"But you must have your supper first, roast beef or something. The shortcake is the dessert." The girl was disturbed by such irregular conduct.

"I want some right now."

She set it before him, a little uneasily.

The girl had been too modest in describing the dish. It was undoubtedly not only the best strawberry shortcake in Arkansas and in the world, but probably nothing beyond the pearly gates could touch it.

The berries were cold and sharp and bright. The crust was flaky and fresh. The cream was rich and plentiful.

He ate the last bite and sat regarding the dish with a thoughtful frown.

"How was it?" the girl asked, when she brought his companion's roast beef.

He pondered his answer, then said slowly, "It tastes moreish."

The waitress took her cue from his manner more than the word, which he said from the roof of his mouth.

"That's the first complaint we've ever had," she said, hurt. "There's nothing the matter with the taste."

"I could have been mistaken," he admitted. "Bring me another one." She brought it and it was eaten.

"Aren't you going to have any dinner?"

"Yes, I'll take strawberry shortcake for dinner. Bring me one."

The girl, wide-eyed and puzzled, brought it, and it was eaten.

"Now I'm to dessert," the man said, "and I'll have some of the strawberry shortcake."

He finished his fourth serving. "I guess I was wrong," he told the girl. "It doesn't taste moreish now."

—June 10, 1947

* * *

The most influential woman in town is the grocer's wife. She may not set the styles or make the ordinances, but she decides what the town eats, which is more important.

To a woman hesitating between two brands of cake flour or canned corn, the grocer has only to say, "My wife uses this." If the buyer frowns over canned or frozen peas, she takes the frosty ones when the grocer says, "We've been using them at home and they're fine."

When the grocer's wife, with a whole storeful of stuff to chose from, settles on a given brand, it's good enough for the customer.

"My wife says" is as weighty in the grocery store as "My husband says" at the study club.

—June 12, 1947

Doorbells and the Outside World

One day a group of little boys was going from house to house collecting old newspapers to sell.

A little fellow who was hardly five went up to a door, looked around puzzled, hesitated, looked again, then walked back to his friends on the sidewalk.

"I didn't know what to do," he said. "They don't have any doorbell or knocker."

When I was child in Missouri I read stories and in those stories people would ring doorbells. I thought the houses must be very elegant to have doorbells and I wondered if I would ever see a house with a doorbell.

The little section of hills and creeks and timber where we lived, including the houses of the people I know and the small town I had been in seemed an island surrounded by the world I read about in books and papers.

Somewhere out there ladies wore beautiful dresses that trailed after them. And they wore white satin slippers. I had never seen any, but I often pretended that my bare feet were white slippers.

Sometimes I would hear older people dourly condemn rich people who spent money for fine clothes, but they were so dazzling in my mind that I could not feel them sinful.

The outside world was a place where poets lived. I had never seen a poet, just as I had never seen a giraffe.

I thought I would like to write poems when I grew up, only I didn't suppose I could go and live in the far-away places where poetry was written.

In time I did see a poet and a giraffe and a house with a doorbell. And, most astonishing, a little boy who is puzzled by a house that has no doorbell.

—July 6, 1947

*   *   *

Churches measure their strength by membership, regardless of the dead timber they drag along.

They might do better to set up a pretty stiff test for membership and allow only those to join who had qualifications.

Maybe require an application vouched for by three members in good standing, a call at the home by a case worker, with a waiting period while the name is being considered.

—July 10, 1947

Pulling and Hauling

Early fall is the time of the pulling and hauling, which reaches a peak soon after the autumnal equinox.

Preachers are home from the lakes and mountains and urging their members to get going after their nice long rest. Clubs have started and phoning committees are on the line saying bring a covered dish.

All the activities which stagnated during the summer are being pulled to their feet and shaken. Committees are called together and alarms sounded.

Get busy on the membership drive, sell tickets, fill one card out and hand the other to a friend, each person bring someone else to the meeting.

Club presidents are charged with making the year a success and that means getting the people out. Any meeting that is well attended is a success.

Meet up with one of the girls who has been to "the group" and what do you ask her? "Was there a good crowd?"

It's a shame, the committee says, for a book reviewer to go to all that work for such a few, a shame for good sermons to fall on empty pews; the musician shouldn't be asked to exert herself for only a dozen, but the strain can be spread to a comfortable thinness if four dozen hear her.

So the theme of the pulling and hauling season is: Get the people out. A leader is weighed by the number of followers he can entice.

But people are annoyingly slow. They are postcarded and telephoned, they are flattered and upbraided, they are appealed to and warned. There ought to be a law that leaders could use the subpoena.

Shuffle the cards, dig out the rummage, wind up and oil the speakers. The days have started downhill into the long dark of the winter solstice.

It's no time to sit home and read a book. Get into your girdle and tight shoes and go out and hear it reviewed.

—October 10, 1947

* * *

The argument that is supposed to clinch any sale is "We sell a lot of them," and the guarantee of quality is "We haven't had any complaints."

A man came to the door urging the purchase of an article because he had sold 500. I could see 500 women all scrubbing the floor with the same mop, a great unseen chorus, stroking in unison.

I thought 500 was a good round number and a shame to spoil it with one more.

—December 27, 1947

74

*   *   *

A group of people working together was asked to say a few words about themselves. Various ones reported positions and places and daring deeds. When it came one woman's turn she said gently, "I don't have a very interesting life. I've been married for most of it."

—January 7, 1948

Great Soul

Gone to join the select company of the great is a little dark-skinned man whose ashes are being borne out to sea by the old sorrowing waters of the Ganges.

In an age when the advanced nations were doing their best to destroy each other and bristling with arms for the task, this little man controlled thousands with a word.

He had none of the outward trappings of power, no gold-braided uniform or polished boots or clanking sword. He was no jowled breast-beater, no frenzied screamer, no job-promiser. His narrow shoulders and thin bony legs wrapped in a piece of homespun did not make an impressive figure.

He sent out no armies or bombing planes.

He held no elections, built up no organization, formed no cabinets, had no committees or key men or press agents or secret policy.

He owned no wealth—to control men because he had their means of life in his hands.

Yet he achieved power to be envied by the worldly and ambitious of his time.

His weapons were simple. They cost no money or materials or man-power or conversion of factories. They were passive resistance, civil disobedience, non-violence—strange weapons in an atomic age.

The little man could stop eating and the British empire quaked in its boots. He went to jail without resistance and injured his jailors more than they did him.

He was a great spiritual cosmopolitan who lived what Christ talked about. He, a Hindu, was the best Christian the world has seen.

He was called "Great Soul" by those who felt the power of his spirit, a power that can not be explained or understood. At a word from him thousands could be quieted or roused to bloodshed.

Yet even he could not make people love one another. He wept at the fresh outbreak of violence following his fast and with tears drank the bitterness of the failure of his life's hope, but in his heart there was nothing but love and pity.

Gandhi's assassin gave him the only thing he lacked to fill out the pattern of the great—martyrdom.

—February 5, 1948

Mass Mind

I am beginning to see what a dangerous thing the mass mind is.

Six months ago, three months, even fewer, I was impervious to the lengthening skirt. I would wear my old clothes, I said, and let the hemline fall where it might.

This superficial show of moral courage was made easy because other women were saying the same thing and wearing what they had.

But now I do not feel comfortable in a short skirt. I regard the knee as a shocking thing and the swelling curve of a calf something to be covered up.

I wish I did not feel this way, but I do, and however shameful my subjugation by the mass mind, I do still recognize truth and can still confess it.

My corruption may have begun with the gift of a new long skirt which a friend cut out and thru a mistake in the pattern, could not wear. It made my other clothes look like museum pieces, in spite of a feverish letting out of hems.

Distressed at my servility of mind, I did not at first mention it, not even to my family. Then in a moment of confidence I told a trusted friend.

"That's exactly the way I feel," and the same unhappy story of insidious bondage burst from her lips. We were emboldened to talk to others, and every one, woman or girl, owned to the same frailty.

What's the matter with us? If a skirt two inches below the kneecap once seemed beautiful, why does it not still? Why this weakness of mind?

Women who are natural againsters, who would not hestitate to offer a contrary opinion, admit they are beginning to feel ill at ease in a short dress.

The old admonition, "If thy skirt offend thee, cut if off," is of no help, for it would only offend the more.

We are victims of the mass mind, a thing as dangerous as an insane criminal and as invulnerable as a ghost.

And if the mass mind can enslave us in the trifling matter of a few inches on the bottom of a skirt, what must it be doing to our attitudes, manners, morals, customs, rules, precedents, our habits and our thinking?

—February 29, 1948

Hat Trimming

My mother went downtown one day this week and bought new trimming for her hat.

It is what one would call a basic hat. She bought it eight years ago for $4 and every time she dips into the millinery marts she comes out with increased regard for the old black sailor.

Her theory about hats is to get a good frame and keep changing the trimming—she says that after all, the shape of her head changes very little from one year to another. Buying a new hat is a great worry, but it's an easy matter to go into a store and pick out a bunch of flowers, a piece of ribbon or veiling, and tack them on before supper.

76

One year the hat was trimmed with folds of wide ribbon, another year with narrow fluted ruching whipped around the outer edge and zig-zagging up and down the crown. It has worn daisies and forget-me-nots, and this year it will be a wreath of blue flowers whose botanical name would embarrass an expert.

But a hat trimmer doesn't have to be a botanist.

—March 26, 1948

No Official Notice

That is a phrase which, the public is beginning to suspect, means, in free translation, I do not choose to see.

A periodic stir is raised about slot machines in places frequented by the prominent and influential. They have been there for years and everybody who goes into the place knows it.

The drive runs its course and the law enforcement officers are interviewed by the press.

Here is where it comes in.

The gentleman being interviewed looks up from his desk at the interesting information that there are allegedly slot machines in the town.

"My office has received no official notice," he says, and the reporter goes back and puts it in the paper.

Or it may be one of the waves of dry enforcement that sweep over the state.

The reporter goes in the official's office with more weary information and asks the usual question.

"What's that?" the official says. "Drinking at the country club? It hasn't been called to my official notice."

There seem to be two theories of law enforcement. One is that officials sit in their offices till a citizen runs in and says he has been shot or robbed or blackmailed.

The other is that it is the duty of law enforcement officials to get around and find out a few facts for themselves instead of waiting to be invited to the cocktail party.

—March 30, 1948

Nice Day

The man opened his eyes and looked around. He did not know the name of this place nor where it was nor how he came here. All he remembered was a great many people somewhere who had talked and argued and disputed.

Perhaps in a moment he would recognize the street. It must be early—that strange luminous yellow-green light—perhaps a storm somewhere. He'd fall in with that character ahead and strike up a conversation.

"Nice day," he began.

The stranger did not reply. He might be hard of hearing.

"A fine morning," he said louder.

The stranger stopped. "In this country," he said, "we do not talk about the weather. If it is a nice day everybody knows it and if it is raining or snowing it can be seen. Our chief statistician estimated the amount of saliva wasted talking about the weather and it was so enormous that everybody met and agreed not to speak of it again."

"Then, what do people talk about?"

"In this country it is not polite to talk to a man just to prevent a silence. It might imply that his thoughts are not worth thinking."

They passed a man sitting a distance back under a tree, rocking and sipping a lemonade beside a record player.

"He's being punished," said the stranger.

"What did he do?"

"Repeated an old joke three times."

"It must be a kind of secret torture—the poor fellow looks pretty miserable."

"He had to make a record of the joke and sit there and listen to it till sundown."

Farther on, two women sat on each side of a glass partition on comfortable divans, with footstools but no magazines or handwork.

"They were quarreling," the stranger said. "They can't hear a word the other is saying, but they have to sit looking at each other till sundown."

"Sundown seems a pretty important time in this country," the man said

"Yes. When sundown comes everybody goes to the edge of town to see it. There is an old saying that the setting sum draws away troubles and drops them into the darkness on the under side of the world."

Something sharp jabbed into the man's ribs and he opened his eyes as a passenger was jostled into a seat beside him on the early morning bus.

"Nice day," he began.

—April 1, 1948

Crowning Joy

(Being the confession of the mother of a large family, now grown).

I accept without bristling the accusation of the psychiatrists that I have hurt my children, and the fact that I also was hurt in the long chain of parent hurt child will not be offered in amerioration.

Wallowing in the luxury of regrets, I ask myself what I have done that might scar my children for life, but seeing them with the fondness of affection I am struck by how superior they are. I long to free them from the mistakes I made in their childhood, or wish that they might know those mistakes I made in their childhood, or wish that they might know those mistakes and let knowing set them free.

It hurts to see a boy happy with his dog. My boys did not have all the dogs they wanted, for reasons that seemed good enough at the time, but I did not understand that a child can learn to love an animal before he can feel human affection.

My boys were sent to their rooms for fighting. It might have been better to let the fighting come to a decision and possible broken limbs. I did not and do not know.

I could have done more to help my children overcome shyness. They seemed such an improvement over my husband and myself that it seemed impossible they could be painfully bashful, but they were.

I worried too much. I was scared the children would catch fire at a picnic, I was afraid they would get tetanus germs in a cut, I was afraid they would drown in swimming. My frantic searchings when they were unexpectedly missing at play were humorless and ludicrous.

It does not comfort me that the mistakes I made were due more to lassitude than to ignorance. I got so tired trying to make people do things that along toward the last two children I gave up. I got tired of bossing, of trying to be God. I let the youngest childen refuse their cod liver oil, tho I earnestly believed it was essential to body growth and half suspected it was meant to put the fear of God in their souls.

I smile with pain when I hear motherhood called the "crowning joy." The words are smug and conceited. No crown is on my head—and remember I said my children were superior.

I bleed for a hundred mistakes. I should have read to them more, given them more music, taught them to use tools and work with their hands, to observe nature. Looking back it seems easy, but I remember that at night I was glad to get them to bed and enjoy a little quiet.

It's all wrong. Nature has made another of her blunders. Children should be born to women at middle age, when they have learned a little something.

—May 9, 1948

To Cap and Gown

When the last child graduates from high school, the question asks itself, "Where has the time gone to?"

She was a pretty baby (I was there and saw her), brown-eyed and earnest, which may have been because she came into the world when it was long-faced from the depression.

There was the Sunday I went off to church with everything as usual and came back to find she had begun to walk and was shuttling between her father and brother and a sack of potatoes, rather aimlessly, it might seem to an outsider, but those who saw it thought it a remarkable performance.

But walking soon became too slow and she began rolling down steps, porch steps and stairs, followed by cut knees and gashed foreheads.

The trolley motorman was one of her early heroes and she would sit on the curb waiting to wave as he passed.

The alley behind the garage was the scene of early locomotive struggles. It was there she learned to roller skate and to ride a bicycle, with her father running along beside her. And it was there she learned to take the car into and out of the garage.

She fetched and carried for her brother in return for the pleasure of his company—ran after balls and drinks of water and something to eat. She tended his lemonade stand when he was tired of it and when he wanted to be Tarzan she obligingly twisted her face into what was purported to an imitation of an ape.

On her first day of school she was extremely doubtful about the value of formal learning, but thought better of it later. In the first grade the teacher let her "play the thimbles and the tangerine" in the "orchestra."

Thru Brownies and Scouting to cutting off her braids and being a giggling Priscilla and her first long dress and high heels and baby sitting and a first job in a store she has come to a cap and gown.

When did she do it? Where has the time gone to?

—May 27, 1948

Family Man

A family man who adds freshness to Father's Day is the returned veteran who has set up a household.

He may not have much of a house, but the household is first class. Fighting the war in far-off places he wondered if he would ever have a household and he vowed and vummed if he ever got back to the girl he had married or was going to marry, he'd sure as thunder (not an exact quotation) set up a household as quick as he could.

And that's what he has gone and done. In trailer or quonset hut or in a hastily thrown up house set in a triple row of like houses he is an exemplary family man.

His foxhole digging serves him well in struggle with the terrain surrounding his dwelling, which can get as muddy as France or Burma or Italy or the lowlands of Holland. He has planted flowers and a garden, set out shrubbery, is making overtures to grass.

Certain Army experiences come in handy in his combat with cockroaches and ants and flies. He has taught his wife how to use mosquito netting, the fine art of diaper folding, and tricks in ironing a shirt. He knows how to run a machine or do a bucket wash, what to iron and what not to iron.

He can turn a few boards into a set of shelves or a writing desk and with a can of paint and an old motor, he has a fancy gadget. Some of his skills may have been learned with grumbling, but he employs them in his household with pride.

He likes to help take care of the children. Out yonder he wasn't sure he'd ever see the baby at home or live to be a father. He has taken the baby to class, held it on his lap at football games, maybe carried it when he went up to get his diploma.

Children are numerous around veterans' houses. In one college settlement cars zipped past at an alarming speed. The fathers didn't complain to the authorities and wait for an article of warning to be put in the paper. They went out and dug several shallow ditches across the streets. On Guadalcanal or somewhere they had learned the value of immediate action and a shovel.

The veteran family man works about his place in old clothes that bear the faint marks of chevrons. He is surrounded by his house, his household, his wife and children, and this, he knows, is the only thing worth fighting a war for.

—June 20, 1948

I Guess I'm Lucky

He stood in front of the talcs and lotions, his young face lean and tense, his hands swift and capable at the cash register.

Without a moment's hesitation he could say if the store had this number film or that magazine. One might think he had always done this.

Perhaps not many who passed thru the busy doors knew that the deft hands had guided planes over the hump into Burma, had pulled the cord that opened white silk above him.

Yet there was something that set him apart. Maybe it was the quiet way he stood. Maybe it was the still look on his face.

For four years he was in the war, flying first a fighter, then a bomber—2,500 hours in the air, 900 in combat. He holds two Distinguished Flying Crosses, two Air Medals, and a Silver Star.

His adventures in the India-China-Burma area would shame Captain Easy. In one of the two times he was forced to bail out, he spent 36 days with the Naga head hunters. Another time he was behind the Japanese lines for 18 days.

The first time, his parachute caught in a tree and he hung there all night and into the next afternoon when he was rescued by terrifying Burmese carrying spears and long corn-knife things—and dressed in the scantiest of G-strings.

The chief locked his fingers together and the flier was sure it meant his death. He offered cigarettes to promote good feeling and groaned to see the savages stick the precious things in their ears and tear them apart.

Living with men whose worth was measured by the heads they took was hardly a tranquil life. A man needed one head to marry, five to sit in the council. A stranger could never know when one of the tribe might need just on more head to complete a project.

81

He saw friends go out who did not return. He himself was listed as missing, and his anxiety sharpened knowing his family would think him dead.

But now he was home, he owned a part of the store, he and his wife were happy in building a home in the country.

"I know I'm lucky," he said, and he must have been thinking of his friends who did not come back, "but it's kind of strange. I get down in the dumps sometimes and just want to walk away and leave everything.

"Of course I won't. I have everything to make me happy and I am happy. It's hard to explain. I'm tickled to death to be here, but I just get spells...Of course I'm awful lucky."

—June 23, 1948

Cow Loose

Emergencies come in towns, but most of them are anticipated and planned for and organized against. People in town know what to do if a building catches on fire or a break comes in a water main or power line, or a tree falls across the street or the cat can't get down off the roof.

They phone somebody and men with trucks and strange tools rush to the scene and apply skilled knowledge.

But one emergency for which the town is unprepared is when a truck has had an accident and a cow is loosed in the streets, as witnessed one day recently.

A young Holstein cow had been derailed on the thorofare that was brimful of people hurrying places in cars and meeting other people hurrying away from the places.

She stepped stiffly on the pavement, obviously puzzled, but trying to adjust her footing to the cement. Then she crossed the sidewalk and found a nice yard of grass and immediately felt on familiar ground.

A small crowd of men had gathered, waving their hands and shooing the cow in all directions. A postman, with mailsack and arms flapping, had turned herdsman and was giving service above and beyond the call of duty.

But when any man attempted to lay hands on her she twisted away with a fluid move of her neck and took another bite of grass. She met her problems simply and in order: She was hungry; here was food. So she ate.

Getting into the truck for an unknown destination had not been her idea in the first place and she felt no responsibility for continuing the journey. But eating was clearly a first purpose. So she ate.

Such an emergency probably does not occur often enough for the tax payers to maintain a cow commissioner with office and staff and stationery, but there surely ought to be somebody a person could phone when a cow gets on the streets.

—July 8, 1948

Complications

The atmosphere is heavy this week with adjectives that have been let loose into it as people haul each other around to gape at the foliage.

The wine satin of oaks, the flamingo pink of maples, the yellow lace of locusts, the gold torch of poplars, mingled with the bronzes and greens cause the vocabulary to get a little out of hand in October.

I can't trust myself to write about it, not yet.

I sit down to the typewriter and say to myself, "Now you must do your fall column today. Don't you know the leaves are at their best and the golden spell may be broken any time?"

"Give me one more day," I answered back, "so I can go out and observe a little more, get fully into the mood."

So I write about something else and wander out again into the adjective-laden air. I drive out and look at a distant blue haze over the tops of daffodil-colored trees. I look down into a ravine at colors like a great paint pot. I breathe hard when I see sunlight on dark red leaves or salmon rose leaves or gold leaves.

I come home dazed and write about tree toads or the political situation. I've breathed too much of that adjective air. Adjectives get into the lungs and all thru the blood and cloud the brain. They're not understood yet, not even by our best doctors.

I'll wait till evening, I say, and go out when the colors have settled.

A big red sun rolls behind the hills and the trees are like girls coming home from a Hallowe'en party, who slip out of their gaudy dresses into pale nightgowns and robes.

The color turns into soft shadows and a veil of smoke blue purple is wound about the rim of the world. Sounds come thru the stillness, isolated and distinct, but not intruding—the caw of a crow, the distant sound of wagon wheels, the drone of a plane, the crow of a rooster, the bawling of a cow.

Back in town women with scarves on their heads are raking leaves. Flame and leaf smoke go up to mingle with the adjectives and cause complications to set in.

I'm not quite myself. I'll have to put that column off another day.

—October 28, 1948

Having Club

It may as well be set down right here so posterity will know the meaning of that phrase, "Having club."

Once a year it comes a woman's turn to have club. She has likely set the date for the season in which her house will be at its best. If she has trouble with heat or has a pretty yard, she wants the club to come in the spring. If her place has winter coziness, she sets the date accordingly.

If she is a curtain washer she jerks them down well ahead of time to insure their being smoothly stiff and uncompromising against the windows.

She sweeps down the cobwebs and cleans out the corners and pushes the furniture around to make the living room look like an auditorium.

So far no great harm has been done. It's a good thing to clean the house now and then.

But she goes about gathering up the things the family dropped down on the nearest surface. She pushes them into drawers or chucks them into boxes or shoves them into the closet and shuts the door.

When she has finished, the tops of the piano and tables look as tho they had been swept by a prairie wind.

The women come and have roll call and read the minutes and listen to the speaker, they drink tea and go uptairs for their wraps and say what a good time they have had and go home.

Then the husband and children come in and begin to ask where their things went to and the woman begins to wonder where she put them—that little picture left on the telephone table, the set of stamps, the notes for a theme.

"I put them somewhere—let's see now." They will all be found in good time, or in time.

The family walks around the house, strangely empty after the neighbor's chairs have been returned. They nibble at the small fancy cookies the chairman of the committee left.

Everybody begins piling things around again and the house begins to look natural. Club has been had.

—December 18, 1948

Time by Noon Shadow

On our mantel is a Waterbury weight clock that my parents bought a few years after their marriage. One of my first memories is of the picture of the little girl in a blue dress holding a basket of flowers and of my father winding the clock every night.

We often neglect to wind it now, for it doesn't matter. We can always set it by one of the electric clocks, alarm clocks, or watches in the house. Or we can tune in the radio for the time or call the girl on the phone.

It is like we were letting the old clock play at keeping time.

But in its younger days it had responsibilities. It was the only timepiece in the house, besides my father's thick silver watch which hung by a shoestring on a nail and was used only when he wore his Sunday clothes.

My mother said that when the clock was new she sat and looked up at it so steadily that she got a cramp in the back of her neck. She thought it was the finest thing she had ever seen.

It was responsible for time and winding it was important. There was no phone, no radio, no rural mail carrier, no close neighbor to supply the time if the clock stopped.

But there was one higher authority—the sun. Before they had a clock, my father had cut a line across the south door sill where the sun stood exactly at noon. My mother cooked dinner by that line and my father went to work and came in by the sun.

They didn't have to be any place at any certain time. The only need they had of knowing the hour was to suit dinner to the coming in from the field. The mark on the door sill was good enough until there was a child who had to be sent to school.

If the clock did stop it was set by the noon shadow on the floor; so it may not always have been on exact Greenwich time. And if it chooses not to go along with our electric clocks, that's its privilege.

—February 20, 1949

No Good Solution

Lawmakers have a tough time with that problem that has no good solution: security for old age.

It is against the laws of nature. For that matter, civilization itself is against the laws of nature.

Man is one of the least forward-looking of the animals. A squirrel buries nuts against the cold, even tho he may forget where he hid them. Birds fly to a warmer climate when they feel winter coming. The squirrel does not say, "Let's enjoy the nice weather. Maybe some nuts will turn up this year—we might be lucky." Nor does the bird try to delude himself that winter may not come, after all.

Certain labor unions are well provided for, and business and industry furnish social security to their employees, all paid by the public in increased prices for goods and services.

Experience has shown that only a few of those who reach the age of 65 are able to take care of themselves. The old do not live with their children as they did in a simpler age. It isn't fashionable to let people starve. Something, then, must be done.

The trouble with social security is that half the population is asked to provide for the other half. It would seem only fair for everybody to be given a retirement pension, since it is public money, whether paid by direct tax levy or by indirect.

When everybody gets an old age retirement it is a matter of you pay for mine and I'll pay for yours, and in that case, each might as well be paying on a little annuity for himself.

That would suggest some kind of a no-profit organization to run an annuity bureau—the government would love to do it—each person putting in money for his own future security, to be refunded to his family if he does not live to the required age.

It would have to be compulsory to be any good. Oh, you wouldn't like to be made to save money for your old age? Neither would I. And wouldn't we raise a squawk if they'd try to make us?

So we exercise our constitutional right to manage oursleves, then when we are old and needy we shiver in our thin clothes and denounce the cruelty of a world that will not help a poor old man.

Well, get your wraps on—this is where we came in. Didn't I say there was no good solution?

—April 10, 1949

Nothing Left

"We simply don't have a thing left after we pay the bills," a woman said to some of her sex thé other day when they had gathered to kill a little time and the talk had gone, as it usually does, to new clothes and re-doing the house.

I think she was feeling poor and abused. It comes from living in a town where untouchables are seen in store windows and where one may observe women in dress shops ordering three changes as lightly as another would ask a pound of hamburger to be sent up.

Nobody reminded the woman of the solid values she tossed off in "after we pay the bills." Perhaps nobody thought of them.

They buy shelter. Her house, set on a pleasant street with paving to keep her out of the mud, is more than comfortable. It has rugs and cushions, easy chairs, music, pictures, and a modern kitchen.

Her food furnishes nourishment plus some luxury for the palate and her clothes are more than the covering demanded by custom and the weather, nothing by Dior, but nice, little numbers from the local stores.

They have a neat but modest family sedan and "the bills" include gasoline to make it run, as well as electricity and gas and coal and water to make the house run.

She has fire and police protection. A quick dialing of the phone, also included in "the bills," will bring either running with open sirens to evict an intruder, prevent a murder, get a cat down from the tree, or put out a blaze. And if damage should be done, the insurance man will come and pay for the loss.

She has mail delivered to her door twice a day and the daily paper thrown on her step.

"The bills" pay her family's share of taxes to support a government in a country which offers more freedom and more comfort and more opportunity than any other place on the earth.

These things would be fabulous wealth in most parts of the world, even much less than her moderate possessions. Yet she lumps off at the gathering of women with "nothing left."

Naturally there is nothing left. They have already paid for everything.

—April 13, 1949

Being Good

One of the heaviest burdens the human race has taken on itself is trying to make each other behave.

The front pages of daily newspapers do not indicate it, but when a person thinks about all that could be done, it is remarkable that people behave as well as they do.

The problem has been approached from every direction and points between. Some are brought into line with the promise of heaven, others are scared with the threat of hell. The approval of one's fellowman works about as often as the fear of his displeasure.

But the greatest factor in the moral behavior of the human animal is himself, an inner feeling of pride and self-respect that makes him behave when he is alone.

It may have grown out of his wish to be thought well of, it may come from his saying, "See, I can be good all by myself. Nobody has to watch me."

The greatest need of every human being is not be liked, but to like himself, to respect himself. And he has to have some reason for doing so, even if it is a flimsy one.

Your man moved by inner pride would not run a red light even if he was sure he was not watched, he would not keep money he found if the owner could be located, and he would not touch another's letters left lying around opened or snoop into closets and drawers.

It is important for a man to win the approval of himself, but it has something to do with his neighbor. He wants to feel equal to the neighbor, superior if possible. He wants his neighbor to like him, anyway to respect him, and how can the neighbor like and respect him if he does not like and respect himself. So he has to set up a code of behavior for himself.

Heaven and hell are far away and uncertain but a man lives with himself every day.

—August 19, 1949

Some Place Else

The only reason we do not have economy in government is because we do not really and sincerely want it.

Forbes Air Force Base is about to be closed or greatly reduced, and the town is hurrying to do something to keep it. We went thru the same anxieties a few years ago when the base was slowed down to walking.

We have all been hollering ourselves hoarse about the way the government is throwing money away in Washington. We shudder at the national debt and wonder if it will ever stop.

Then somebody in Washington tries to do something about it. Secretary of Defense Louis Johnson plans to save $50,000,000 a year. He, says there is "terrific waste and extravagance" in the military establishments.

The brave secretary has a tough job on his hands, assuming that all the adjacent towns are putting up the fight that Topeka is.

Meetings are held and a congressman is called home to talk it over. (I believe he campaigned earnestly for economy). I have no doubt that any of Topeka's business men would deplore the waste of public money. They have learned about money and economics by taking risks themselves in their own business.

The mayor said he would be "severely disappointed," and he said that of course all communities would like a service base near by. "But on the other hand," he said, "I am sure most people are equally anxious to see government spending curtailed."

Sure they are, but they want it curtailed some place else. They are like the plump woman who wanted to reduce and was willing to go on a diet provided it didn't interfere with her meals.

—August 27, 1949

With Willard in 1936.

My parents, Jacob and Margaret
Bennington - 1940.

Our children, Willard B. and Dorothy.

Willard B. - His first suit.

Dorothy - in coat her grandmother made.

E.B. Greene and grandchildren.

With Willard B. and Dorothy - 1931.

1940's

Christmas 1945 - Willard B. home from World War II, with Willard, my mother and Dorothy holding Midnight.

With Everett Rich at Emporia State University - 1958.

Judges of the Bugs Bunny coloring contest, 1952 - Louise Roote and Dorthea Pellett.

My mother and her grandchildren Melissa and David Hanger, Christmas, 1957.

5

Willard and I at a Flint Hills outing.

th Preston and Anna Hale - celebrating both our 40th wedding anniversaries - 1958.

Mary Turkington presenting award for outstanding Kansas woman journalist from Theta Sigma Phi - 1959.

With Thomas Hart Benton at Washburn University - 1961.

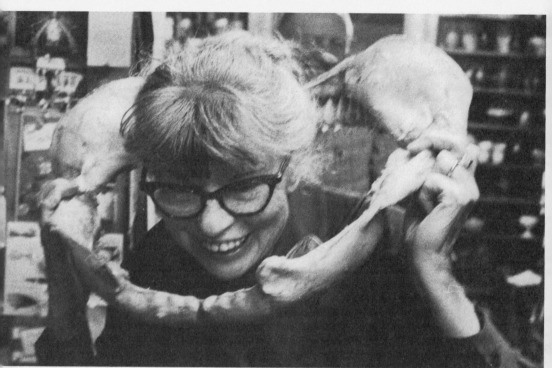

...ing on a shark's jaw.

...h Bill Mitchell in a T-shirt given to me by Mayor Bill McCormick (center) - "Peggy,
the flint hills forever".

Willard B. home from Korean War with daughter Joyce - 1951.

Willard B. and wife Marilyn with granddaughter April in Hawaii - 1978.

III
1950-1959

In the Beginning

Most of the years I have been writing a column I have handed out suggestions every New Year tending toward the elevation of manners or morals and the general improvement and well being of the human race.

The chief value of the same was probably that it lifted my own spirits and at the same time filled my space in the paper for a day.

I have more confidence in my readers now. I am sure they yearn toward goodness as much as this column does and are finding as many ways to hack thru the tangles that spring up in their path.

This I do believe: That the thing a man most earnestly longs for in his heart, not always the thing he says he wants or thinks he wants, but what he actually desires, he will achieve.

A person says he would like to learn to play the piano—there's nothing he'd rather do. Yet he continues to spend his evenings with the radio or movies or games, while the piano stands untouched.

The truth is that he does not want to play the piano as much as he wants to enjoy easy diversion.

A person says he would love to write a book but he doesn't have the time. Whoever burns to write will write, if he has to write in prison, or at night by a candle, or over a sandwich at noon.

The understanding of oneself is the key to more tranquil living. To understand one's own deep desires, and one's own baseness, and not to make excuses, or cover up, or deny, or tint with rosiness, but to recognize

99

and acknowledge them and to know they are a part of all men—that is to have a solid foundation to build on. It is the beginning of a dependable structure.

My wish for 1950 is that you will make it a good year for yourselves.

—January 1, 1950

Troubled Typewriter

This typewriter has been acting strange. It keeps trying to get away.

I'll be writing and after a while will notice it has moved toward the end of the desk, edging along when I am not looking. As nearly as I understand the term, its behavior points to a persecution complex.

I yank it back to the center of the desk and in no time it is on its way again, headed straight south toward the wall. If it was moving toward the north there might be some reasonable explanation of magnetized metal. (I guess you're right. That does seem a little far-fetched.)

But straight south leads right into the wall and I sometimes have the feeling that what it wants is to crash head on into the plaster and do away with itself. There was that time it tried to, though nothing could be proved and it had the appearance of an accident.

It was left standing on the little drop-leaf table one night, solid and firm as far as could be determined, but the next morning it was found on the floor with its big framework bone broken.

As I said, it could have been an accident. The cat could have told what happened — she was in the house — but she just looked a little more mysterious than usual and said nothing.

This desk is strong and sturdy. The machine can not turn it over. No dangerous means are within reach — no acids that might corrode the keys, no matches, no blunt instruments. Nothing is left but escape.

The poor thing is obviously disturbed. Of late its spelling is sometimes erratic, its judgment often impaired — it hesitates when confronted with a series whether to use commas or semi-colons — and, I am sorry to say, that twice this month it has used a plural verb with a singular subject.

The machine has been overhauled and touched up. Some of its parts may have been left out, but perhaps it has grown melancholy from the weariness of daily duty, so that it seems better to try to make it to the wall and dash its keys out than to go on and on like this.

—January 20, 1950

*   *   *

There seems to be a rule about clerks. The higher the floor, the cooler. Girls in the basement call you honey and can't do enough for you, but the honey congeals in the chill of the fifth floor.

—March 16, 1950

100

Free Agent

A small boy in the neighborhood is entering into the state of becoming a free agent.

His mother used to haul him in from play and set him down for his piano practice. She sat by him and told him when he could stop and go out to play again. He had few good words for music.

Then he had a birthday and she told him he was old enough to decide whether he wanted to take piano lessons and he could do as he pleased about it. Her first surprise was when he elected to keep on with his music. The second was his voluntary practice.

But a little cloud has come into his world and casts its shadow. He is tasting the sharp sweetness of being a free agent and beginning to realize with the psalmist that man is born to tears and sorrow.

He must either be forced to do another person's bidding or assume the pain of self-discipline.

It will not be any easier as he becomes older. Social custom, will, conscience, instinct, desire, duty, will battle with each other for his soul. The battle will never be ended, for the losers will camp on his flank and lick their wounds for a fresh attack.

To a child's eye the great wonderful free world of grown-ups is eminently desirable. There a person does as he pleases, nobody to boss him. He comes when he wants to come and goes when he wants to go.

And when he has been battered in that great wonderful free world for a few decades he will look back wistfully to childhood, that fabulous land where a boy's only problem was to outwit his mother about piano practicing.

—April 16, 1950

From The Mists

Standing with relatives of other babies, my husband and I saw our first grandchild. There didn't look to be a quarter's worth of difference among the dozen babies ranged in a row. All were similar shapes of red, all were dressed alike, lying in identical baskets at the Parkview Hospital in Manhattan, Kansas.

But each person at the window was eagerly intent on the child that was a part of his own self.

The self is the core of living and the protection of it the first instinct. That self comes from two parents, four grandparents, eight great-grandparents, spreading back in an increasing wedge into the mysterious mists of life's beginning.

And with the coming of children and grandchildren the wedge begins on the other side to spread into the mysterious mists of life's ending.

A self comes from myriad lives whose roots are entangled in the roots of the world. They are a vast network springing from far continents, from lands that may lie buried under the sea, from the sea itself.

The roots were kept alive through bitter hungers and numbing colds.

101

They were pulled through famine and fire and flood and pestilence and war and sickness and accident and chance. They grew in dark caves, on hot deserts and bleak plains.

That long march of lives was dear to me as I looked at our day-old granddaughter, who had joined the roots of her parents in a new self. I gave thanks for the hardihood of those lives, however they had walked and whatever kind of skin covered them. I was mindful of the fierce instinct of self that had brought their seed safely to the middle of the twentieth century.

If any one of them had faltered or failed, Joyce Ann Greene could not have lain there vigorous and kicking, with every contour and color exactly as they were. Welcome into the world, Joyce Ann. It's a bit cluttered up, I'm afraid, but you come of a long line that has survived worse than this.

—May 7, 1950

*   *   *

One of my mother's first memories is of a man riding a white horse and carrying a flag at the Centennial celebration in 1876. She and her sister had new red and white striped calico dresses. The flag had thirty-seven stars.

That was the year she cut impromptu bangs on herself and her sister, in imitation of the pretty schoolteacher who boarded with the family. It was her first year in school, which she loved. Now in her seventies she recites poems and entertains herself by reading the encyclopedia.

And she has a precision with words. Downtown her eye was caught by a lavender print and after a little resisting she bought a length. "I didn't need a new dress," she said, "but I wanted one."

—May 15, 1950

Cost

"They're only fifty cents - they ought to be worth that," a woman said, deciding to buy a set of salad molds.

They were bulky. They would not stack together. She would not use them once a month and they would take up more room in her cupboards than the pans she uses every day. She would have been ahead if she had thrown the half dollar away, along with the penny tax that went with it.

For every gain there is a loss, for every object acquired there is a price and we are acquiring so fast that it is a question whether or not we are not losing more than we are gaining.

First, there is the cost in money, and money is not just folding paper. It is a piece of your life, if you earned it. Then there is the space that an article occupies, the time spent taking care of it, the time spent getting it out and putting it away. Put everything in the house through a grilling test and much would come up with a minus.

Take a white linen suit. It costs something, but add the hours spent ironing it and it would be no bargain if it was free.

102

There's that bag for sprinkling clothes, hardly worth getting out for each laundry, putting away afterwards and storing between times. A towel in the basket is just as useful.

Racks for drinking glasses to clamp on card tables — getting them out, putting them away uses time and space. Valuable jewelry is a load on the owner's mind, and if it is not valuable it is still a load on the dressing table.

Ornaments are looked at and they ought to be worth seeing. Too many are not. If packed away, they occupy space. Too many books, records, pictures, hats, dresses, kitchen gadgets — many are not worth the time and attention and space they require.

All cost a piece of your life. Stacks of odd dishes and packed together so closely in cupboards that it takes a series of liftings to liberate the orange squeezer or the measuring cups.

We lose money and time and peace of mind and quietness when we buy something that is not worth owning. Only the most beautiful, the most useful and the most priced possessions are worth keeping. An article costs more than the price tag it carries.

—June 20, 1950

Tired

A brisk young man's remark that you have to have something to do to keep from being tired may be nearer the truth than it sounds.

He has a gasoline and bait station. When business is popping, cars waiting to be filled, fishermen standing in line for minnows, he is full of energy, but on rainy days when nobody seems to want gasoline or on quiet mid-week days, he comes home tired.

Quite a good many people who say they are tired would be speaking more accurately if they said they were bored. Boredom probably causes more weariness than overexertion.

Let a woman have an interesting evening to look ahead to and she can fly through her work as light-footed as a ballerina, when otherwise she would be sighing over the phone by mid-afternoon that she was all worn out.

A girl can dance till the pale hours of the morning and never lose her sparkle, but if she had to stand a couple of hours in an evening and do the ironing she would complain that her feet were killing her.

A man can carry fifty pounds of hunting clothes and a heavy gun all day, tramp up and down mountains, carry a deer on his shoulders and feel fine, when at home he would come from the office all worn out from sitting at a desk, talking to a few people and dictating some letters.

A boy can work all day, carrying rocks and boards to build a fort in the back yard but ask him to carry out the trash and he hasn't the strength to lift a waste basket.

The whole family can jump at the work like a ship's crew ordered to man the guns if it is suggested they could all go to the show if the dishes were done. And who hasn't known of a person, languishing in bed with a minor complaint, having a sudden recovery at the prospect of something interesting to do?

The young man was more profound than he intended to be when he said that you have to have something to do to keep from getting tired.

—August 8, 1950

Golden Aisles

You don't have to wait until you achieve heaven to walk up and down the golden aisles. Just get out into the country where the roads are lined with sunflowers.

Never have the sunflowers been taller or sturdier, bigger or yellower. Moving through the golden lanes in the shimmering golden air with the golden sunlight hot on your skin, you could step right into the pavilion of heaven and never know when the boundary was crossed.

Little streams and draws are bordered with gold and here and there solid fields paved with sunflowers reach back to the misty blue horizon.

Spotting the gold are clumps of purple and blue. Thistle and ironweed and the range of late summer flowers have never been brighter. The goldenrod flaunts a purer yellow than the sunflower and the gay feather has never been gayer.

For the quick of eye the blue purple of wild grapes and the dark burgundy of elderberries offer a glimpse of richness tucked in among the shining leaves of the hedge. And far above hangs the blue, blue sky, with white clouds skimming along like little skiffs.

Before I can be persuaded to leave these golden aisles of Kansas, and book passage to heaven, I will want to know whether heaven has blue skies high over the golden streets, whether the gold will be splotched with amethyst and ruby and sapphire and jade to relieve the monotony, and whether there will be rare small fruits to reach up and pick.

If I learn there is nothing to expect but gold and pearl and jasper I will elect to stay right here among these golden aisles.

—September 10, 1950

Winds of Time

The winds of time are blowing across the world. They come from the far mists of the first beginning. They blow beyond the world to the unseen, unknown mists of time's ending.

They blow clean and strong over the world, winnowing hope from discouragement, separating faith from despair, sweeping away the rust of failures and the broken bits of dreams.

Time sweeps ahead, never back. It leaves old sorrows to soak into the earth and clears a space to start building for the new year.

To cling to the past is to suffer slow decay. It is tacit admission that the best of life is over, that the peak is past, that the memory of the past is more pleasant than imagination of the future.

Whether you are running up a golden hill straight into the blue sky, or

104

are on the steep down grade with the mists in sight, there is no place to go but ahead.

If only a few years remain, they are all the more precious. Spend them as a traveler crossing the desert spends his one canteen of water. If you have many to spend, make them buy what you most desire.

Time is the rich treasure, the years of life, which turn out to be not years, but days doled out in trickling hours and in dropping minutes.

No polished stone or hidden chest can compare with the richness of time, and each person is given a portion for his own.

He can not stop time while he sits down to think and ponder how it shall be spent. It flows on like the taxi meter, whether he is still or moving. The winds of time are blowing across the world and they do not stop.

—January 2, 1951

Sewing Club

Government was originally designed to see that people lived together peaceably and that justice was done. How far it has deviated from that purpose can be illustrated by a little story about a woman's club.

Some years ago a group of neighborhood women thought, since they all liked to sew, that it would be nice to meet at each others' houses and sew together. They wore whatever they would be wearing at home and dropped in at whatever hour was convenient.

After a while they said they probably ought to elect a president, and they included a vice-president in case the president became sick. Someone said they ought to have a secretary to keep track of the meetings, and maybe dues—say 50 cents a year for some little things they might want.

They met several afternoons, then one of the women decided it would be nice to have something to eat. She served cake and coffee. After that each hostess felt she ought to serve refreshments. One by one they added a salad or pie, than a hot dish, then a hot dish plus dessert. One hostess suggested they come a little earlier and have lunch. The idea took hold. It turned into a luncheon club.

They elected a program chairman and raised the dues to a dollar a year, then two dollars. They decided to have a guest day and to make printed yearbooks, for some of the new members did not care much about sewing and the club had added piano playing and book reviewing. They said those who wanted to sew could bring their sewing.

They adopted a constitution and by-laws, added a parliamentarian and a treasurer, raised the dues to four dollars and started keeping their hats on.

Roll calls were responded to with favorite movie actors, favorite animals, favorite poems, favorite flowers and favorite birds. The club appointed membership and publicity and decorating and program committees and distributed a little news sheet each month to let each other know what was going on.

Once a month they played bridge and every fall they had a rummage sale.

The other day when some of the older members were reminiscing about the beginning of the club, a newer member exclaimed, "You mean this used to be a sewing club!"

Nobody brought their sewing any more.

—February 18, 1951

Out to Sea

A big Navy vessel sailed this month from a western harbor and a report has come from an interested bystander who was carrying a baby.

The baby had been wakened early that morning and there was hurrying around to get a certain Metalsmith Second Class (but strictly first class to the two bystanders) aboard. (He would't have missed the cruise for anything!) The woman went home to feed the baby, then drove back at sailing time.

The men and officers were lined up on the deck for inspection and the band was playing. They tooted and beat out the stirring strains of "Sailing, Sailing," "Anchors Aweigh," and "Auld Lang Syne."

The woman ran down the dock with the baby and someone who knew them pointed out the voyager they were looking for. They waved at him and a dozen men waved back. Everybody waved to everybody.

At the dramatic moment the Admiral appeared and was piped on board with all the trimmings (the Metalsmith had gotten himself on board somewhat less conspicuously) and the tugs began dragging the monster slowly out to sea.

It did not seem to the woman with the baby that the ship was moving at all, then the water began widening and the great hulk swayed as it lumbered away. The woman kept waving till the ship was turned around and the men could not see the shore. They were at attention facing the sea.

The Admiral's wife got into her Cadillac and was driven away. The Metalsmith's wife got into her Chevvie, tied the baby into her riding chair, and drove back home.

—March 18, 1951

Immortality

Man's last try for immortality is the granite tombstone, the grave vault of "permanent" metal.

He hopes for heaven, yet he clings to his earthly identity, appalled at giving up the dear familiarity of his body and his name for an unseen and unknown existence.

He wants his body preserved, his name seen and spoken. He wants those who will come into the cemetery in ten years, twenty, a hundred, five hundred, to spell his name out of the stone and to say it with the warm breath of life. It will link him to the living.

For these he employs the most enduring metal, the hardest granite.

Yet it is only a whisper more or a whisper less in the long calendar of time. Whether a pine box or a copper, the earth will have its own—in time, in time. And it has the time to wait.

If all who ever lived on the earth had been laid in their own little plots with a marker, the earth would probably be covered with graves and there would be no room for anything else.

But the earth has business with the living and cannot afford space for all the dead. It will take care of its needs in time, in time.

Here and there are old cemeteries, little early country burying places, being closed in by grass or persimmons or oak sprouts that have grown bolder as the little plot was less defended. In time the relatives will have died, the stones fallen down, the mounds leveled, and the earth will again have its way. Trees and shrubs and wild flowers and grass will grow again.

And what better cemetery could there be, what gentler resting place, than a sea of grass, unmarked?

—May 27, 1951

Back Home

"I'd never go back to a place like that," you hear people say. "If it flooded once, it will flood again and you'd never know how soon."

Nevertheless, many are going back. Barefooted, in jeans, they are working. Furniture is piled in the yard, mattresses laid out to dry, clothes hung over lines and flood-matted fences. In many yards fires are burning.

The scenes are like descriptions of people who have gone back to their bombed homes. Stunned, they move slowly thru the waste and destruction, seeing dear and familiar things broken and coated with mud.

The wrecked homes reveal more ruin and destruction. A grim spirit hangs on. Stubbornness might be another word, but it is hard to know where courage and stubborness divide or where judgment comes in.

Cleaning up goes on slowly. Where does a person start when muddy debris litters his yard and is flung against his house?

The house itself has a hole in one side, the porch is tipsy, the floors bulge, the plaster is off the lower walls. Ironic is a painting hanging in one house, of a girl standing on the grassy banks of a pretty blue lake, ethereal and serene in a filmy white dress, a flower-trimmed, ribboned hat held in her hand. The picture is untouched by mud.

The glass is out of the windows. What does a person do first? How can he mend a hole in his house, straighten its crooked leaning, and put on new plaster? And how can he wash and clean and scrub a house that is so mortally wounded?

The people move slowly, lifting mud with a shovel and throwing it someplace else. They carry things out to dry. That is something they can do. And toward evening they stand in their doorways or sit on their porches, not looking tragic, not looking heartsick, but expressionless.

When a person has shoveled mud out of his home and seen the ruin of beloved possessions, he is beyond emotion. He finds a comfort in home, his own home that he has come back to.

Where else would he go?

—August 3, 1951

Sailor With Seabag

The day her sailor husband was expected home a young woman put on the same pink skirt, pale blue sweater and pink neck scarf she wore the morning she drove him to the ship.

They stood in the middle of the bus depot with their baby, a little circle of radiance in the dark shadows of people around them, as the sun, breaking through open leaves, illumined a spot of blue shade to golden green.

In his slim sailor suit, topped by the white hat that angled across his dark hair, he looked even taller than his six feet. He picked up his seabag and lifted it to his shoulder.

Once before, his mother had seen him coming home with a seabag on his shoulder and had later wanted him to go back outside so she could take a picture.

"Me lift that thing again!" he protested.

A tall sailor carrying a seabag on his shoulder is a picture of grace in motion that needs sketching, that needs catching with a movie camera, anyway photographing.

But perhaps memory is sharpened by a flashing glimpse of an easy motion that picks up a tightly packed and locked heavy cloth sack and in the same movement rests it on his shoulders as he walks away with it. Perhaps imagination is better served by that glimpse than by motion arrested and deadened by a camera. The picture in the mind is forever flowing.

"I love to see a sailor with a seabag on his shoulder," his mother murmured.

"I don't," said his wife. "He looks better with a baby."

He agreed and happily exchanged his seabag for his little girl.

—November 11, 1951

Monterey

It is impossible to put the charm of Monterey, Mexico, on paper. Altho it was just an ordinary day we spent there, yet it seemed like something played on a stage, some program rehearsed for a holiday.

The city is full of open plazas, with statuary in the center, palms and flowers, and seats everywhere. Joe Lee would love Monterey.

People spend the evening in the plaza as they spend the evening at the movies in other towns. They sit with ease, talking, looking, listening, or just sitting—not tense or expectant or waiting, just sitting easy.

Yet the plaza is not without business. Dozens of barefooted little boys, with a box slung across their shoulders, importune loungers to have their shoes shined for a nickel, or even better, for a dime.

108

Others offer bouquets of roses, gardenias or little tied nosegays for the same money. Little girls dart about asking for a nickel please. Horse-drawn taxis, a single dim light standing above the dashboard, offer trips around the city.

Bands of musicians in big sombreros and short jackets stroll thru the plazas, playing for anyone who will pay them, or just playing—they would sing for the music even if there were no pesos. They surrounded as we sat on a bench.

"You like 'Cielito Lindo'?" they asked.

We said we liked "Cielito Lindo."

They sang it in voices that lay like silver on the night, fingers moving smoothly over guitar strings, their faces illumined by song, an unforget-table melody of flowers and stars and music.

Along in the evening began the parade of the young people around the broad outer walk of the plaza, the girls outside, the young men inside, walking in opposite directions. They walked round and round, in twos and threes and groups, for more than an hour, eyeing each other discreetly and occasionally pairing off for dates.

The parade takes place three times a week. It is an old Spanish custom.

The music kept on, heard at various distances as the plaza emptied, and we went to sleep with "Santa Lucia" coming from melodious tenors in a open-air beer garden.

It seemed too much to be going on naturally and we half expected a cur-tain to go down and dissolve the flowers and palms and music, the happy, unstrained faces, the ease and relaxation.

In the morning a man with a long grass broom was sweeping the plaza to prepare it for another day.

—December 15, 1951

Sheets

Of all the delights of shopping, buying sheets in the white goods sales surely comes first — it is important that they be bought in the sales, to en-joy the added satisfaction of thrift. Sheets are something a woman can smooth and arrange with the joy a miser gives to fingering his money.

From the days when cave men bedded down on a pile of pine needles or leaves or dried weeds to the esthetic refinements of sheets must be quite a span. You can say this for man: he has the capacity for luxury.

When I was a child in Missouri sheets were made by sewing together two strips of unbleached muslin down the center and hemming the ends. They were too short and too narrow, leaving little to tuck under and nothing to fold back.

Later we bought sheeting by the yard — ten yards for four sheets, still too skimpy. I wondered why the catalogs did not encourage the making of longer sheets by quoting prices of an eleven or twelve-yard bolt.

My own evolution in sheets somewhat paralleled the cave ancestor's.

Gradually I bought larger ones, first longer, then wider, and then I changed from muslin to percale.

I once heard a woman say of her new hat, "It pleases me to think that no woman in town has a better hat," meaning "a more expensive hat." The enjoyment of fine sheets is not competitive. No woman glares at another who owns the same brand. On the contrary, it is a pleasure to find such a woman, the way one stamp collector likes to meet another.

Like a farmer with full silos or a bin bulging with corn is a woman who has a closetful of sheets, smooth percale, 90 by 108, gleaming white with a pair or two of pastels, if the taste runs to color.

Unfold one — almost as light as silk and as crackly as taffeta. Plenty to fold under the sides. Plenty to tuck in at the foot. Plenty to turn back over the covers. Stretch out between them at night, confident they will stay in place.

A lineful of sheets billowing in the wind and soaking up the freshness of the sun and air. Bring them in, fold them, and lay them away. What fragrance in a bottle could touch the smell of sheets fresh off the line.

—February 10, 1952

Hand to the Plow

Thursday morning in Abilene Dwight Eisenhower gave a performance that marks him as a major leaguer. He stood up before several hundred members of the press and radio and answered questions with force and conviction and sincerity.

He stood on the stage at the Plaza Theater in front of radio and newsreel and television microphones, while out in the theater rows of cameras, with a definite hint of guns, were turned on him. He was flanked at each side of the stage by reclining cameramen, cameras were operating at the rear, and fierce lights beamed on him.

The general was surrounded. The stage must have been something of a "high plateau of tension" to him—that was a phrase he used to describe the present world situation—but he occupied it with the ease of chatting on his front porch.

Even more formidable than the batteries of microphones and cameras were the several hundred men and women waiting to ask him questions, some of them designed to trip him.

But he did not trip. He did not evade, he did not strain to please, and he did not yield to any temptation to give snappy, quotable answers that might be taken up as slogans.

Expressing the view of the inter-involvement of problems, he said: "Whenever you try to segregate something and call it an issue, you find it infringing upon something else equally important and each of them finally seems to become as broad as life itself."

He would not be one likely to make impulsive or expedient promises, nor to make decisions without knowing all the facts. He did not promise an end to the Korean War or even that he could see an immediate end.

He refused to be involved in personalities or race questions. Bearing himself with good humor, with dignity, and with confidence, he won the respect and admiration of the horde of news reporters, who greeted many answers with warm applause.

—June 7, 1952

Distinguished Relatives

You don't have to search the libraries or hunt among old tombstones to find yourself a noted ancestor. Nor to brag if your family tree has a signer or a judge or diplomat.

That is a very small matter in the fierce light of the ages. For every man living on earth today has distinguished ancestors.

They distinguished themselves by staying alive when it would have been easier to die. Every person living comes from an unbroken chain of men and women who lived thru fire and flood and famine and cold and pestilence and pillage and war and wild beasts.

Long ages ago when life flowed out of the ancient seas the most hardy and the most adaptable survived on land.

Some forms of life branched out into experiments that failed. Those chains became extinct. Others tried to go back to the good old days of life in the water when food swam into their mouths. They failed, too, and became extinct.

But our ancestors were hardy pioneers. They learned to be wise and wary, to have a sharp eye for a jungle cat or an enemy's spear. They distinguished themselves by not eating poisonous plants or taking pneumonia in a damp cave.

They lived.

They survived the invading seas, not once, but many times, as they crept over the land for periods of millions of years. Sixty per cent of the earth's surface was buried in the Ordovician waters, but your folks and my folks were safe in the hills.

Every feminine ancestor survived the dangerous ordeal of childbirth, and every ancestor came thru the even more dangerous ordeal of infancy.

Man has done wonderful things, from the wheel to television, from the alphabet to a symphony, but the most wonderful of all was to survive.

So the next time somebody tells about an ancestor who crossed the ocean in the Mayflower or the prairies in a covered wagon, you can say that away back about 450 million years ago your great-great grandpappy crawled out of the sea and learned to live on land.

—June 8, 1952

David and the Golden Haze

Every tree has been a golden raintree and the ground is covered with golden rain.

The best was in our own backyard, on the patio with our grandson. It was as warm as a spring evening. The flagstones were covered with fresh yellow leaves and yellow leaves fell slowly from the limbs above.

111

David, fresh from his nap, was still drowsy enough to sit and look at the falling leaves. A two-year-old boy will sit quietly on laps only when he is about to go to sleep or when he has just awakened. His head lay against my shoulder, his big brown eyes dreamy, his golden skin pink from sleep.

It was the perfect moment. In a little while darkness would cover up the golden haze, and in a little while David would be bounding away in his fierce quest for knowledge, asking swiftly and eagerly, "Wha's that? Tell me, wha's that?"

—October 29, 1952

Of Time and Years

Some of the most intense feelings of my childhood were at the approach of a new year.

Watching the old year out was a rite that I observed alone and in silence, with a rug pushed against the crack under the door so my parents would think I had gone to bed.

I read my favorite poetry and copied down some of the best-loved verses, as tho they somehow had to be written and preserved in a cornerstone of the old year.

I wrote the names of all the family, particularly my own, "for the last time" that year. I went thru this solemn ritual with an awkward anticlimax, for the old year hung on and refused to give up just because I had finished the writing. I started it over again, listening for the clock and hoping to be on the last dot as it began striking.

And when the new year came, it came silently. There was no radio to bring the shouts of celebrants into the house, no neighbors closer than a quarter of a mile, and they were all undoubtedly asleep.

My parents and the rest of the family had gone to bed at the usual 9 or 10 o'clock and there was no sound inside the house but of quiet breathing; and no sound outside but the wind.

The year came silently, but it burst on me with the violence of resurrection. Never since has it seemed so dramatic. Shouting and crowds and horns and bells and whistles have never stirred me with the awe of time as sitting alone shivering—the heater in the next room was bedded down for the night—while I wrote words on paper and listened for the clock to strike.

It was a Waterbury weight clock with a picture on the front, of a little girl in a blue dress picking flowers. It is standing on our mantel at this moment and I expect to hear it strike midnight tonight, but without any writing of names and without the drama of renascence.

For time is no longer a thing that moves slowly and goldenly thru a year to creep to a majestic peak on a midnight in December.

It is now jet-propelled.

—December 31, 1952

*   *   *

Best comment about Gabriel Heatter came from my mother: "His talking sounds like such hard work."

Clif Stratton snapped his cigar lighter. Nothing happened.

"I feel like the foolish virgin," he said.

—January 15, 1953

Reader

My mother is a modest woman and would never claim this distinction for herself, but I think she must surely be the greatest living authority on "Little Brown Bruno."

It happens to be a favorite book of her two great-grandchildren. They hunt up the volume and take it to her as soon as they are in the house, sitting beside her in her rocking chair as she reads.

I would not say that she has dived any great depth into the historical bibliography or psychological implications or social inferences of the popular tome.

Nor does she spend any great amount of time analyzing the succession of events that enmesh the hero in his formative years—the gray hen, the cat and kittens, the eagle, the donkey, the baby, the housewife—and contribute to his character development.

She does not apply a Freudian yardstick to his frustrations nor prod into his infancy to search for unhappy stimuli. She does not try to make anything out of his uneasiness in the presence of his maternal parent or of his overdependence on the favorable opinion of his contemporaries.

But there is one thing she sure can do and no fooling: she can anticipate every movement and flicker and feeling and thought of the adolescent Bruno even before she turns the page.

Joyce often assists in the reading. She assigns one page of the book to her great-grandmother and takes the other herself.

With a low mumbling she runs her finger along the lines, turns the page when she is ready, and begins reading again.

She is becoming quite an authority, too.

—February 8, 1953

*   *   *

Some feel honored when they are put at the table where the best linen and china are laid. That table is for visiting guests of honor, for new acquaintances, and old enemies.

People who are set down at the best table are those that the hostess wishes to compliment, to impress, or to give no grounds for criticism.

The ones who are really honored are those who are set at a table where the dishes do not match and the eating utensils are recruited from the kitchen.

They are the true and trusted friends who do not need to be complimented or impressed and who would never think of criticising.

And therefore, the most honored.

—March 1, 1953

* * *

A man who is on an austere diet of mostly plain green stuff says he should think that a cow, after a summer of nothing but plain grass in the pasture, would welcome slaughter.

—May 12, 1953

Peace with the Earth

How quiet it is in the tenements of the dead,
families together in their small houses,
neighbors across the way,
all making their peace with the earth.

Debtor and creditor alike...
no anxiety for money lent or money owed,
anxiety making its peace with the earth.

The pious, the wanton, the drunkard, the frugal and
spendthrift, the wise and the foolish,
all under the same green quilt.
Conflicts and passions have melted into the earth.

The rich man, for all his grand marble and
stately mausoleum
sleeps in the same narrow bed
as the one who lies beneath
the wooden marker too faded to be read,
making their peace with the earth.

But once life ran hot in their blood.
One bought and sold. One was powerful.
One was favored with beauty and grace.
One was wild and wilful. One was born to pain.
They loved and hated, wept, erred, sorrowed and rejoiced.

Life was a little span between two mysteries,
a waking between two sleeps,
a brief neon glow on the long dark line
that disappears at each end into the mists,
and the beginning can not be seen
nor the end.

114

But that brief glow
when it shines and flames
can light a fire that defies the mists
and makes its own peace with the earth.

—May 30, 1953

Dukie and the Bright Century

"Dukie" Jones, our young red-headed neighbor, has uttered the most touching expression yet heard about the Centennial. Dukie is nine. In deep sadness he spoke to his mother of his unhappy relation to history — too young to grow a beard for this Centennial and before another hundred years passed he would be dead.

You just wait, Dukie. This is only the beginning of a century thick with centennials. You'll see dozens of them and grow enough beard to upholster a davenport.

The year 1966 will be the centennial of the first railroad in Topeka—the Union Pacific. You will be 21, and able to flaunt a flaming red beard that will excite wonder and admiration. Three years later the Santa Fe will have its centennial—and will try to outdo the U.P. You will be 27—and off on another beard-growing spree.

Washburn College will be coming along with a centennial. Every year in the next century is bound to be a centennial of something or other. Even in this first year, which is just the start, 246 separate events and celebrations are listed between April 25 and September 30.

Along in the seventies the towns father west will start having them...Hutchinson, Dodge City, Garden City, Great Bend, Liberal, Salina, Russell, Hays, Abilene—and I bet you these towns will put on a real rip-roarer of a Centennial. The year 1872 found the railroad reaching clear across the state—that will be something to celebrate. You'll be 27 in 1972.

The year 2000 ought to be some fine celebrating just on general principles, a good round-numbered year like that. And four years later Topeka will be having its sesquicentennial. Only a few old dodders will be left from this celebration and the new generations will be having a real streamlined 21st century blowout.

—May 14, 1954

What Comes Natural

David, taken to the circus by his grandfather, showed more interest in the food vendors than in the performers. He was pleased by the animals and approving of the whole thing, but a four-year-old is still living in the magic of creation and too unfamiliar with reality to be a top circus fan.

He is not impressed by a man riding a bicycle 20 feet above the ground, with a pole across his shoulder on each end of which other men are riding bicycles or beating eggs or engaged in some activity. So far as he knows, anybody could do it. He accepts is as a natural phenomenon, as he accepts all other things he sees daily.

A man and a woman are swinging. That interests him because he likes to swing, but there is nothing unusual about it even when they fly thru the air, grasp hands, and return to their own perches. He believes any person could do it.

A man tosses a dozen objects up, keeping them all in the air. He has seen a person catch one ball and he sees no difference between one and 10. A catch is a catch.

A girl stood on a big ball and maneuvered it up and down inclines and did a juggling act at the same time. David was interested but not impressed. He had his eyes on the ice cream man while fellows were flipping nimbly about the springboards, being bounced up high and into a chair that was all ready for them.

A man supported three other men on his shoulders. Just another thing that people do. David has been watching the strange goings-on of people ever since his interest spread in widening circles around his crib. Whatever he sees he assumes to be normal activity, and he accepts it as reasonable. There is no reality or unreality, no normal and no unusual. He is living in the first days of creation.

An older child, one who has lived long enough to understand the ways of the world, is the real circus enthusiast.

—July 7, 1954

Birthday

Today is David's fifth birthday.

I treasure a moment when he accepted me on common ground, not as one of the elders who order his life, no matter how benignly, but as an equal.

It was after one of the rains. He had scooped up mud and put it in a wooden box that was outside in the back yard. There was plenty of mud on a little bare space north of the house.

He had on shoes and stockings. I remarked conversationally, when he asked me to come out and see his mud, that when I was a child I liked to walk in mud with my bare feet. I described the cool feeling as it squashed between the toes.

It sounded like tall talk to a town child who always wears shoes, tho he may go without a shirt.

"Show me, grandmamma," he said.

I kicked off my shoes and we cautiously approached the mud. David had some doubt that it was anything he ought to do, or even something that he would like to do.

But soon he was stepping in the deepest and softest places and saying, just as children have probably said for hundreds of years when they saw mud covering their feet, "Look, I've got black shoes!"

116

When we were washing our feet with the hose, he gave a delightful little shiver and asked in the low, excited tone of a fellow-conspirator, "What would our mothers think if they saw us?"

Both our mothers were in the house but they didn't see us. They were busy with grown-up things like sewing.

—July 14, 1955

Bully

Going thru old letters I came across one written a good many year ago by Niles C. Endsley of Alton, Kan. He was commenting on my current campaign to try to get people to call a bull a bull not The Gentleman Cow, The Male, or The Cow's Husband, which were some of the names that prudish woman have used to designate the head of the herd.

Women who would say "rooster" a dozen times a day simply couldn't bear to hear the word "bull." Apparently a male chicken was not indelicate.

That was one movement I had a lot of support in, and I will have to conclude that it must have had some success. At least I never hear a bull called by any of those pretty-pretty names any more.

Mr. Endsley was telling about the name of a town that was changed thru prudery. He wrote:

"When my mother came to Alton the buffalo and Indians were often seen on the present townsite. The name of the town then was Bull City. Its founder, Gen. Hiram Bull, was very prominent and was state representative from Osborne County.

"When they were framing a herd law for Kansas, he told the Legislature he would vote for the bill providing they would let the bulls run at large. General Bull kept several varieties of wild animals in a park on his place in the adjoining town. It was one of these that finally killed him, a pet elk.

A few years after the death of the General, the wife of a business man of the town, one of those aesthetic sort of women who blushed every time she said the town's name, started a movement to change it.

"And strange to say, she got the job done. A few years later she was gone, but the town was Alton then and the old-timers wondered why they had been such fools."

"As I read my letter over it makes me think of Teddy Roosevelt's favorite remark, 'It's bully!'"

—September 23, 1955

Gentlemen Preferred

It is a bad time of year for it, but, judging from the ads of rooms for rent, ladies can sleep in the streets. Gentlemen are preferred as paying guests.

The reasons given privately, are that women are always washing out things and hanging them around limp and dripping. It gives the house a draped, closed look.

117

Then they come home sometimes with that far-away shine in their eyes and say they would like to do a little cooking. It is the domestic instinct coming to the surface. Most of the time it is under excellent control, but when it emerges it must be satisfied.

The roomer comes in with a package of cream cheese, an assortment of vegetables, a parcel of shrimp and a few other goodies which she turns into a meal. But she needs the use of the stove and sink to do it.

Then company is always coming in, running up the stairs, running down again and yoo-hooing through the windows.

Men, say the room-renting people, have no domestic instincts that compel them to cook a little bite for themselves and wash out a few things, though of late there have been some dacron or orlon or nylon shirts hung dripping overnight.

And they rarely have company, but leave the house quietly and come in quietly. And if they don't come in at all, the renters do not need to feel any concern or responsibility.

These reasons which seem to make women less preferred as roomers are, whether admitted or not, the same reasons why employers usually pay them a little less than they do men.

Women, they argue, can live on less. They can do their own washing, they can mend and cook and even save money on clothes with a little sewing.

Also, they get married and quit any time. But the man who gets married is for sure not quitting his job, unless he gets a better one or marries an heiress.

All these things are behind that two-line ad which says: "Nice comfortable room, near bus. Gentleman."

—November 25, 1955

* * *

Several years ago when my granddaughter Melissa was three or four she was at our house when Mrs. Frank Boyd was here. Later she took a great shine to Mamie, but was shy at first acquaintance. When Mrs. Boyd asked, "Do you like me?" Melissa answered, "I don't know yet."

—January 31, 1956

Gulf

Teenagers have one term with which they can wither a middleaged adult. And that is "It's too new for them," said with a kind of sorrowful and patient tolerance.

The middle-ager, most likely a parent, feels like flying two ways at once. He thinks maybe he ought to like some new things, such as Elvis Presley, just to prove that his mind is not boarded down and nailed shut. And at the same time he is annoyed at the illogical assumption that anything which is new is good.

There is a considerable gulf between the two ages. The youth cannot understand the older person because he has not traveled far enough yet to reach many different planes. And the older one often fails to understand the younger because he has forgotten how it feels to be young.

Parents, having themselves arrived at the age when physical resources must be conserved—when they know it is wiser to go to bed early than to wear themselves out dancing the night away, when they know that saving money is a greater satisfaction than spending it, and when they regard work as more pleasure than play—think along the lines of care and caution.

Their advice to the young is modeled on the basis of these mature discoveries. But urging them on a child is like asking him to start a journey and end it without seeing any of the interesting sights along the way.

It is like advising them to go to the fair, look around a little and come home without knowing the tinkling rhythm of the merry-go-round, without feeling the thrills and excitement of the loop-a-plane and octopus, without savoring the delectable taste of pink cotton candy and a footlong hot dog, without that anticipation of spicy worldliness of walking boldy into the side show the barker warns is only for the broad-minded.

The young person could be told that these things are not worth standing around and wearing oneself out, but he would not be convinced. He could be told that going to bed early and avoiding strenuous exercise were insurance for a sound old age, but he's not interested in old age.

These things he will know in time, along with the satisfaction of work and saving money, but he wants the pleasure of crossing over the gulf and discovering them for himself.

—June 10, 1956

*   *   *

It was fancy eating at the Alice B. Toklas dinner given by Frances McKenna and Gene DeGruson last week. All the dishes were from the Toklas cook book. The only thing they regretted was that Frances started making the yogurt too late for it to "set".

Guests ate Onion Soup, Salad Aphrodite, Veal Marengo, Green Peas a'la Goodwife, Potatoes Mousselines, Garnished Salted Bread of Bugey, Flaming Peaches, Coffee and Cointreau. It was hard the next day to get back to hamburger.

—Feburary 9, 1957

Poor Dear Fern

Some years ago in a spirit of adventure I answered one of those marriage bureau ads that promised to send a list of handsome, rich men eager to marry. I said I was Fern Dawson. I didn't want anyone panting up to the door and discovering I was a middle-aged fraud who already had a husband and two children.

119

I was sent some literature with dandy descriptions of wealthy, handsome, fun-loving gentlemen who wanted to meet some nice woman and settle down. No names or addresses were given.

But the bureau had another list of men, much, much handsomer and far, far richer which could be sent for ten dollars, five dollars now and five when "married or suited." Presumably they did not think it likely that a person would be both.

If I would fill in the enclosed blank and send five dollars I would immediately receive the list. And my name would also be put on a select list to be sent to a choice collection of gentlemen.

I was to fill in my name, address, age, weight, height (ten years ago people were not obsessed with bust measurements), color of eyes and hair, religion, occupation, amount of property and income, marital status, children, and a brief description of the kind of gentlemen I wanted to correspond with. And I must sign a statement affirming that I was free to marry.

I did not write them any further, although I continued for some time to get lists of charming descriptions which did not seem to fit either my own husband or those of my friends. How could it be that these gems of manhood had been overlooked and were now so eager to be caught when all the accumulated experience points to the fact that an ordinary run-of-the-mill man is hard to get?

I planned, should anyone ever come to the door and ask for Fern Dawson, to take on a sad look and sigh, "Poor dear Fern. The last anyone ever saw of her she was heading toward the creek and all they ever found was her shoes."

Then I would add, sorrowfully, "She hadn't been—well—quite right since she wrote to some matrimonial agency. She seemed to brood about it a lot. . . . Say, you wouldn't be connected with it, would you? If you are, I understand the authorities want to question you."

I worked up such a good scene that I was almost sorry nobody ever came.

—June 2, 1957

Honeysuckle

Honeysuckle grows on a fence in my backyard between the house and the garage. During the day as I work at the sink I see it through the kitchen window, modest white and yellow flowers among a mass of green leaves, simple flowers that would hardly be noticed. When I return home in the night I walk along the row of honeysuckle.

There is something about the scent of honeysuckle, coming on it suddenly in the darkness, that stabs the senses. Why does the scent of a flower, the call of a bird, a full moon in a veil of mist, a silent flowing river bring a tumult of joy and sadness all mixed together?

The scent of honeysuckle in the dark calls up memories of years long gone, memories that fly through the mind in a kaleidoscope of change from peak to peak—the pleasure, the pain, the errors, regret, all mingled together in a feeling that is none of them and all of them.

It is as though the sensual pleasure of a scent in the warm summer night dips deep into the well of the mind to draw up fragments of living. It is the sorrow of time passing like a river, flowing the sweet scent away, flowing our lives away. One stands alone, a stranger on the earth, and the sweetness of the night is like a wind that comes and goes and plays a strange music that fades away.

What is there in a simple yellow and white flower that can be so moving?

—June 15, 1957

Lesson in Astronomy

I feel that I have done poorly in my first opportunity of the Geophysical Year to dessiminate scientific knowledge.

Our granddaughter Joyce, who lives in Manhattan and has been visiting us, was lying across the bed and looking out the window at the big round moon.

"What holds the moon in the sky, grandmother?" she asked.

Casting about for ways to explain to a seven-year-old child something I did not well understand myself, I held forth, in words I hoped she could understand, about gravitation, the planets, the solar system, satellites, rotation and revolution.

"Oh, you mean there's a long invisible string that holds the moon?" she asked.

I backed up and tried again. I took a round perfume bottle and rotated it while moving it around a light bulb which had been designated as the sun. I tried to explain that the moon moved around the earth and the earth moved around the sun.

The poets set down their awe of the spacious firmament on high. David exclaimed, "When I consider the heavens, the work of thy fingers, the moon and the stars which thou hast ordained, what is man that thou are mindful of him?"

Yet man is the most marvelous of all, for he questiones and seeks and pursues knowledge, from childhood onward.

The ancients made up their own stories to fit what they observed of heavenly bodies, and they were probably just as believable to the young as what scientists hold to be accurate information in this 20th century.

Joyce summed it up: "The moon just stays up there because that's its home."

Okay. Next question.

—July 21, 1957

*   *   *

Our granddaughter Joyce, who is seven, stayed with us a while during vacation and had a sweet way of leaving little "surprises" around the house, neatly written little notes or pictures she had made.

One was a poinsettia made of paper with modeling clay, signed and labeled. At one side she had written "Made in Japan."

Her explanation: "Well, about everything you get has that on it."

—January 9, 1958

Give It Time

A new production in London of the Greek play "Lysistrata" has been able to sidestep the censor because it is more than 2,000 years old. That seems to make morals a matter of relativity. What is a scandal when it is happening may become a romantic love story a few centuries later, by which time the principals are no longer around.

An out-of-bounds romance, like whisky and good furniture, seems to mellow with age. Romantic ladies of the past, such as Helen and Cleopatra, may have been clucked at by their contemporaries, but their indiscretions have become classic after the passing of centuries.

Illegitimacy is very poorly regarded when it is current, so poorly that governments offer what protection they can and mothers give up their babies to spare them the humiliation of not having two parents properly married to each other.

But time does a nice glossing job, and in six to ten generations an illegitimate ancestor can become one that is bragged about, if his parents were illustrious enough, or if he was brilliant enough.

It may be of small comfort to persons suffering from unconventionality to reflect that in time they will not be criticized or snubbed or discriminated against, for by then it will be too late.

Adam and Eve, who never had the papers, are well thought of today.

—January 18, 1958

Theology and the Young

I wish our grandchildren's parents would hurry home from Florida and tell Melissa about God. She exhausted my slight knowledge of the subject at the first sitting.

I make an effort to answer all their questions, but find myself running behind. It is easier to talk to David about suns and planets and light years then to discuss theology with Melissa.

The other day after she had sat quietly in the small rocker in my writing room, she suddenly asked, "How many gods are there, grandmother?" I was writing about taxation and the question caught me unprepared.

She made a prefectly logical explanation of her question: "People say that God is inside you, but there'd have to be a lot of gods or they would be in pieces." In other words, If there was only one God, and if God was inside everybody, he would have to be divided into many parts.

I made several attempts to explain the abstract idea of a god, but got nowhere. She herself interrupted to supply the details. "God lives up in the clouds," she said impatiently. "Everybody knows that."

The legend of the old man with the long beard who lives in heaven, a location somewhere in the sky, persists even in the atomic age. I tried to talk about love and goodness and the mysterious force that made the earth and the heavens and all the wonderful things everywhere, birds and flowers and squirrels and trees.

In the end I gave up.

I remember that her mother once stumped me with the question, "Who borned God?" Let her do the answering now.

—March 30, 1958

Conversation

It's no wonder women talk more than men. They have so many more things to talk about.

Men meet and after they have exchanged opinions about business and politics, discussed the baseball standings and the mileage they are getting on their cars, and recounted a few new jokes, they've had it and they move on.

When men fare forth for the day they leave their personal and domestic life behind. No man would think of discussing with another man the material for his new suit and whether it is to be single or double breasted and the size of the lapels.

Nor would he dream of confiding in a brother that he has to wear one-piece underwear because he can't keep his shorts up, or that his wife sits in front of the television all day listening to those drippy soap operas while the house is a mess.

But women have hundreds of things to talk about. They can discuss at great length the details of furnishing in every room of the house, how they are getting on with their painting lessons, how much money their team has raised for the church and what to do for ants in the kitchen.

Talk about their children can be extended to book length. Women used to mention such simple things as whether a child has cut all his teeth, but now they discuss whether or not a child should be taken to the guidance center for psychiatric help.

Women talk of clothes and patterns and sewing and the meeting of the club and of how their husbands sit down with the paper, then when dinner is announced they go in to the bathroom to wash up. They talk about how nice the lilacs are this year and how miserable they were all winter when they had that virus and of their pleasures at finding another Westward Ho tumbler.

They talk about the books they have read and the movies they have seen and the chemise dresses and the cute material they found for a playsuit.

123

The subject of clothes is never exhausted and the speakers seem never to be.

Business and politics and the ball games and jokes—one would think that men would become so tired of those topics that they would break down and let it out that the begonia was about to bloom.

—May 18, 1958

Words on Walls

The museum at the Kansas State Historical Society has several rooms furnished in various periods. A kitchen is papered with newspapers, one being a section from the Chase County Leader of, I believe, March 6, 1886.

It is a kitchen with a bed in one corner, a rocking chair, a table, a stove, and in one corner a sink with a pump. That pump seems too much of a luxury to go with a newsprint-papered kitchen, but it seems so only because, when we had such a room on my parents' farm in Missouri, we pulled the water from the well with a rope and pulley and a wooden bucket.

One of the agonies of my childhood was when my mother pasted the last installment of a continued story on the kitchen, the story side against the wall.

The story was "The Laurel Bush," so named because the plot of the story was woven around the fact that a letter was lost under a laurel bush and caused a long separation and sad resignation between the hero and heroine.

The man, a schoolmaster, went away because he thought the woman, a seamstress or governess, had not answered a letter he wrote saying if she would consider him as a life partner, to write him. If not, spare him the sorrow of a letter.

He thought she had not answered and she, poor soul, thought he had gone off and never bothered to write her a word. So instead of writing and saying did you get my letter, he pined for 20 years. And she, instead of writing and saying why haven't you written, you big cluck, did likewise.

Well, he came back to see her and the first thing he noticed was the thimble on her finger. That was the last word I ever read. And the misery it caused me can only be remembered at this late date, not understood.

I felt sure they would make up somehow and that everything would be explained—she had found the lost letter years afterwards—but I was torn with pain not to be in on the finish. I looked tensely at the sheet pasted against the wall, thinking that by looking I might see through the paper.

A woman at the museum said that her mother always pasted the papers upside down to keep her daughter from spending so much time reading them.

—May 31, 1958

Willard

The years of a marriage fuse two persons into a oneness, a new compound in which the two elements do not lose their identity.

Willard, my husband, was quiet and calm and self-effacing, yet people immediately felt the deep strength and stern honesty ingrained in his fiber.

His brother Churchill said: "In those qualities which count in the worth of a man he was preeminent — integrity, courage both moral and physical, reliability, gentleness to those about him. He has been a sort of Rock of Gibraltar in the Greene family, a fact which we knew even if we did not embarrass him by telling him so."

He was a rock of strength in his own family. Others might falter or waver, be flighty or depressed; he kept the same even level of courage and dependability.

Courage is often thought of as spectacular. His was for daily use. I hardly know which took more courage, for him to whack our big Holstein bull over the head with a milk stool or to milk a dozen to 20 cows twice a day. Once when my wedding ring rolled through a hole in the kitchen floor of our farmhouse, he took a light and crawled through chinks in the foundation and rescued it. I thought that took great courage.

I don't remember that he was ever afraid of anything, whether it was a strange noise in the house, a clap of thunder at night, a hard job or an unpleasant duty.

With a simple and direct joy he never lost, he marvelled at the stars and the infinity of space, at the story of time in the rocks. He was entranced by the mysteries of the earth, would wake at night at the honk of wild geese, and could be overcome with tenderness at a sad little story about someone he did not know.

Music was his delight—he had a nice tenor voice and whistled melodiously — and he loved the blend of voices in a great choir or the sweetness of strings.

His opinions were sharp and positive, but he never confused opinion with fact. He never assumed attitudes; he could be nothing but himself. He had a fierce love of freedom in all its expressions, and the equality of men was not just a fancy phrase to him, but a part of his nature. He treated all men alike and it was impossible for him to deviate an inch from an opinion or action he thought was right.

We learned, or should have, to accept his knowledge, for in an argument he was always correct. He knew words, meanings, and his spelling was as certain as the dictionary's. He wrote with force and clarity, and with originality. His ideas were always his own.

Trips were a joy, but because of the scenery and the people, for he never failed to pass up exotic items on a menu and look for chicken fried steak. He loved the ocean, and loved it best when the waves were high and wild. His great wish and hope was to cross it, not high above it in a plane, but feeling its heave and swell under him and hearing its crash and roar.

He gave love and loyalty and patience and kindness to us all and asked little for himself. Once he defined Americanism as: "A respect for the rights and dignity of others without exaggerating the importance of our own, for of course over-emphasis of our own rights limits those of our fellow citizens."

I am afraid he would not like this column. He felt strongly that personal and family matters should rarely be mentioned.

—October 27, 1959

IV
1960-1969

Silence

"Another thing to remember about silence is that nobody can repeat it to mean something else." So says the Atchison Globe, whose wisdom over the years is memorable. I would not dispute the sage Globe, only add a postscript.

True, silence can not be repeated, but things can be inferred from it, and misconstrued.

If a friend's reputation is being torn to shreds in your presence and you sit there without opening your mouth, it could reasonably be thought that you concurred.

If somebody in the office promotes expensive presents for the boss and you make no objections at the time, it would be thought that you agreed. The old saying is that silence gives consent.

When a young man asks, "May I kiss you?" and the girl says nothing, he would be very backward if he waited for a verbal yes. Maybe he would be backward if he asked instead of taking.

There are mass silences, such as greet the sergeant when he asks for volunteers, but these have no reason to be misconstrued. They mean nobody wants to do it.

The most misconstrued case of mass silence is undoubtedly in the women's clubs when the president asks if there are any objections and not a voice is raised. But the minute the meeting adjourns there is buzzing as the members air their objections in twos and threes.

—March 6, 1960

Weather Warning

When the Weather Bureau sees a storm headed this way it warns the people.

So I feel I would be doing less than my duty if I did not alert women to the dangers of something that is now menacing the female population of the East Coast.

It is the beehive hairdo described lately in the New York Times. I saw a picture of it at Catherine Hathaway's, but she has not had any calls from any of her customers for the new style.

The Hair is swirled upward in a movement like a road winding up the side of a steep mountain, rising higher and higher with each loop and ending far up on top in a hole that looks like a crater.

It may be the hole in the head you hear so much about nowadays.

Directions are to "comb forehead section into a slush bang and hold in place with scotch tape." In the meantime the hair is wound on "magnetic curlers," spoon-like devices that look as though they belonged in a plumber's kit.

Mindful of what a Kansas wind would do to a beehive hairdo, I am issuing a weather warning as it swirls this way.

There is one thing you can say about the beehive hair-do, and it's worth saying: you can see that it has been combed.

—March 26, 1960

Too Wild

So the sunflower is too wild for the centennial emblem? That is the word that came from the centennial board a few days ago.

I wouldn't have supposed that they were so enervated by the winter as all that. Grass is about here and perhaps they should have waited till they had a taste of spring greens. There's nothing like the first greens to rid a person of the winter doldrums.

The sunflower, that rugged, free, golden glory of a flower that blooms everywhere without being asked, is ditched for a mild imitation called the glorioso golden daisy.

Why, the very name sunflower has more glorioso than all the daisies in the land. It was not without a friend at the meeting. He got on his feet and protested. The answer was, "But this daisy lends itself to planting in flower boxes and gardens."

Flower boxes! Great jumping jupiter! Celebrating a century of ruggedness in a flower box! The garden clubs can't wait to get hold of some seed.

A hundred years of Kansas:

Plainsmen who never saw a flower box.

Bullwhackers who never laid eyes on a sprinkling can.

Homesteaders who lived in dugouts.

128

Farmers who watched insects devour every green blade in sight, who saw a brass sun curl the green corn and turn it brown, who breathed dirt and came through.

Men who survived land-grabbers, opportunists, goat-gland doctors, sockless radicals, theiving officials, hypo-critical temperance politicians, banquet oratory and campaign speeches.

They endured and came through the century—to celebrate their survival with daisies in a flower box.

Anyway, we are already the sunflower state. We have gone around for years impressing on a lukewarm nation that we are the sunflower state. It has even been set to a tune and sung. Alf Landon spread it all around in 1936.

If it's golden glorioso that's wanted, look along the roadsides when they are turned to golden aisles. Not all the flower boxes in the state could match the golden glory of one mile of sunflowers.

And nobody has to plant them. They're there already, waiting to come up.

My heart is out there with those bold gold flowers. I must pause a while till it comes back.

—April 3, 1960

Bazaar

When the little town of Bazaar in Chase County celebrates the centennial of its post office on April 16 I hope to be there.

I first knew Bazaar as the place where I addressed letters to a young man I had fallen in love with almost from our first meeting, and it seemed a fair and favored spot.

Later when I married him I found that it was indeed. I remember the kind of neighbors who added to my first happiness, and how they came to help me the first time I had silo fillers.

I remember swimming in the South Fork with neighbor women and girls, often with a baby in a basket on the bank, like a little Moses, but not afloat. Often my husband and I would swim at our own old swimming hole on our farm.

I remember many things from the years we lived in our house on the hill, a big house that burned on December 18, 1925. It held many happy memories and some sad memories. The neighbors came with bedding and furniture and other essentials and fixed us up for housekeeping in the tenant house the very day of the fire, which was fortunately early in the morning.

Our children were born at Bazaar, at our home. Nobody ever thought of going to the hospital, which was off at Emporia, just to have a baby. We took our boy there when he broke his arm, and my husband came to

Topeka when the bull batted him against the corn crib, but having a baby was home work.

People were born at home and they died at home.

For 15 years I lived encircled by the gentle slopes and curves of the Flint Hills and saw them change from brown to green and back to tawny rose and often to white. But I did not know until I left, what an indelible part of my life they had become.

Upstairs is a quilt the Bazaar women made for me when I left, each block embroidered with the name of the woman who made it.

These things will always draw me back, for there near the little town among the hills is much of my life.

—April 10, 1960

Not an Easy Thing to Face

A lot of us are as bumbling as the government, but the consequences are of less importance. At this moment in history, our government seems to be in plenty of trouble, and in an embarrassing situation in front of the world, because of the U-2 incident.

Spies are nothing new certainly, or, to put it more pleasantly, the intelligence service. But being caught and admitting you were spying is not an easy thing to face.

Khrushchev is making the most of it, as we would if the situation was reversed. Can you imagine the fuss and furor if a Russian plane, equipped with cameras and radar and a dozen other fact-recording instruments, had been shot down over this country?

How can nations expect to make any honest agreements around a table when it so obvious that they distrust each other? We are suspicious of the Russians and they are suspicious of us. If they read our magazines bristling with stories of military power, they could surely conclude that we are war-minded.

Yet the truth is that the people of this country, almost every person of them, longs passionately for peace, for a world where their children and grandchildren can live without fear of the bomb.

And I do not doubt that the people of Russia yearn just as earnestly for peace.

How to secure that peace and the guarantee that life will not be destroyed is the problem of the times. Why should it be so hard to obtain that which everybody wants.

As one who has bumbled much, I am sympathetic for the crisis the government has gotten itself into. Wouldn't you have thought, with so much at stake, that the intelligence service might have waited till the summit conference was over?

—May 15, 1960

Special Interest Wedding

I have a special interest in the wedding of Kelly Deeter and Marjorie Jones in Kansas City this afternoon.

Kelly was the baby in the radio serial, "The Coleman Family," which I wrote for WIBW in 1935-37. It was sponsored by the Coleman Lamp and Stove Co. in Wichita. For a half hour every Sunday at 1 p.m. events transpired around a farm family we called the Colemans.

It was hard times on the farm, but John Coleman, the son (Tom McGinnis) up and married Margaret (Helen Deeter) anyway. What's a little old depression when you're in the notion of marrying? Helen had just married Vail Deeter. Her nice singing voice as well as her nice speaking voice got the part for her.

John and Margaret lived with the old folks for a while, then fitted up a discarded boxcar for a home. A young couple I knew in Chase county had done that. It was no trouble at all to fill an episode with talk of decorating and fixing up.

Time went on and John and Margaret were expecting. Imagine my surprise when I discoverd that Helen and Vail were also expecting. I wrote the thing as we went along, not knowing what was going to happen two Sundays ahead.

We timed the birth of the Coleman baby to coincide with the birth of the Deeter baby and Helen's absence from the show. She practically had two babies—one on the radio and one in the hospital.

The Deeters named their baby Kelly. We had a contest for a name for the Coleman baby—a lamp was the prize, I believe—and the winning name was Paul Byron.

Kelly came to rehearsals and performances in a basket and he made sounds on the show several times. He really can be said to have made his radio debut at the age of six weeks.

A lot of water has gone down the Kaw since then and here is Kelly getting married himself.

—June 11, 1960

The Loved Quadrangle

A hundred years is a long time. Many men and women lived and worked and dared and hoped and died and triumphed to bring this State of Kansas up to where it stands in this year of our Lord 1961. Kansas is many things to many people.

To Eastern writers it is a breezy place in the Midwest where odd characters and folksy people can be located.

It is the old Mennonite saying the way to be successful at farming was to "plow the dew under," meaning to arise early and work long hours.

It is a woman taking a width out of her calico wedding dress to line the coffin for her first baby, which her husband buried in a corner of their homestead.

131

It is mud dripping into a sod house after a heavy rain.

It is prairie homesteaders dried and parched from sun and wind and loneliness.

It is a benevolent Frenchman who believed passionately in the equality of man, coming to the state to establish a silk factory for which he raised the silkworms.

It is a cathedral rising on the plains.

It is cultured and educated men from Sweden creating a bit of their homeland and establishing a college.

It is cattle bawling and cowboys singing along the trails from Texas. It is gamblers and dance hall girls and cattle rustlers and horse thieves and men who took the law into their own hands.

It is the weary and improvident and hopeful and adventurous finding homes.

It is idealistic and educated New Englanders fighting with Bibles and rifles.

It is men who started a newspaper before there was a town.

It is a golden sea of wheat under a blue sky, a sea of waving grass, buffalo blackening the plains, hills covered with cattle.

It is farm houses, rural mail boxes, country schools, village churches.

It is a young man making the first airplane flight in a pasture, jets trailing silver ribbons.

It is a brassy summer sky, winter blizzards, sullen flooded rivers, dry streams and the sweetest days and gentlest breezes this side of heaven.

And most of all it is the loved quadrangle that is our home.

—January 28, 1961

Rich Gift

My mother, Margaret Bennington, died last month at the age of 92. Richer than any other thing she could have given me were the years I spent with her.

In my childhood we were together in the garden, the woods, the pastures. I went with her to set hens, to gather wild berries, to pull bark from the elm to color Easter eggs. She taught me to milk, to cook, to sew, to play the organ, but all the time I was learning much more from her than these things.

Some persons grow more difficult as they grow older, but it was not so with my mother, who only seemed to flower in added grace. She did not meet her later years with resignation or resentment or resistance or with inner panic. They were still the main deep current of her life, flowing smooth and still.

We did not think of her as old, for she was always a vital and active member of the family, cherished by all, not dutifully, but happily. People felt comfortable in her presence. Her great-grandchildren loved her and would go straight to her the minute they entered the house. They called her "Grand Becky."

She never needed to be soothed or calmed or comforted, for she was the most serene person in the house. Not once did she ever indulge in self pity and I am sure she felt none. She bore her sorrows quietly and wanted nothing for herself. Instead she would ask several times a day, "Is there something I can do for you?"

She read papers, magazines, books encyclopedias, song books, sometimes would sing softly to herself or play hymns on the piano. She could recall poems she learned in school. Anagrams was her favorite game. She cared nothing for radio and television.

Born in the days of real pioneering, she wove linsey cloth from wool off her father's sheep, worked indoors and out, looked after the house when the younger children were born and learned early to take responsibility. She has sewed and knitted for three generations of children and mended everything that got torn or broken. She pieced quilts, braided and crocheted rugs. Eight years ago when she broke her hip, she pieced two quilts and embroidered Christmas gifts while she was sitting out the time in a wheel chair.

She liked to keep busy. Her greatest pleasure was growing flowers, and she left shrubs and plants to bloom wherever she lived.

Though many hours were spent looking at old greeting cards, pictures and letters, she did not live in the past or reminisce. She never belonged to a club, played a game of cards, used lipstick or went to a beauty parlor. But the inner values that guided her were never out of date.

I have never known the least shade of insincerity in her smile or word or act. She was never anything but her natural self, and that self was goodness, not a showy goodness to be laid aside and taken up, but a steady, unchanging light that still shines. The years spent with her were a rich gift.

—February 4, 1962

* * *

The courage and skill and calmness and stamina of Lt. Col. John H. Glenn Jr. are of heroic quality and are rightly honored. He was willing to risk his life to venture into the mysterious sea of outer space. He has earned honor and acclaim.

But my awe is for the scientists who could chart the path of the rocket ahead of time and know where it would be at any minute, and who could put it together in the first place. The whole thing in its vastness and knowledge and precision is another garland on the brow of Man, who pulled himself out of the caves into outer space.

Will man ever get to the moon, or to other planets of our solar system? If he does, will he ever get back?

—February 23, 1962

Goodness and Mathematics

I have had to revise, as I went along, some of the ideas I held about the world and goodness when I was a child.

In my early thinking, there was no doubt of the ultimate goal of mankind, really a double goal in our family—to prepare for heaven and do well in mathematics. The mathematics was the idea of my father.

Goodness seemed the aim of man. There was little economic push back in the hills where I grew up. No one had much money, no one we knew. Some had bigger farms than others, and some in the lowest fringe had no farms at all.

I was well versed, from listening to lengthy sermons, on original sin and man's downfall, I was also led to assume that the older a person was the better he became. The elderly were practically saints, and parents must be without fault, for they knew all the answers about what was right and what was wrong.

So it must be only the young that were sinful. They seemed to cause most of the trouble. There wasn't much to do about it but wait till we grew up. In the meantime, a peach switch was of some help.

I had another concept of time and goodness. As goodness progressed in each individual, it also progressed, I thought, in each generation. The human race, I did not doubt, was growing better all the time.

The opinion must have been formed from hearing about the way Christians were treated in earlier times. Around where we lived it was perfectly safe to be a Christian. Indeed, to declare himself as one increased man's stature in the eyes of his neighbors and his standing in the community. That is, if he was "a professing Christian."

Total goodness did not seem to be coming at any great rate of speed, but I looked ahead confidently to seeing it in my later years, which then seemed far away. I expected to be pitched headlong into the millennium, with Satan chained and harmless.

I caught on eventually that original sin pops out in each generation and that mass evil can happen in any century. But I still believe that goodness is the chief aim of man. And of course mathematics, too. Everybody should know how to figure.

—August 12, 1962

* * *

When you hear a woman bragging that she wears a size eight, you don't need to ask which it is, a dress or a shoe.

—October 4, 1962

Burning Leaves

Cautioning against burning leaves, the mayor mentioned the danger if smoke gets in the eyes, the danger of an accident with the car. Then he said this: "Foul smelling smoke makes a neighborhood nuisance and asphalt streets are damaged from heat."

134

Skimming the Cream

I am not prepared to argue about asphalt, but I am about the smell of burning leaves. Why, just everybody runs outdoors and sniffs nostalgically when a pile of leaves is ignited. The smell makes one remember every joy and sorrow, every pain and every rapture. They all become one and are fused in timeless remembering.

Well, goodness sakes, I wrote a poem about it once a long time ago and I'll just set it down here for Mr. Wright to read. Also, for one of the boys on the city desk. He said to me the other day, "Peggy, you've not whomped up a poem for quite a while."

I think he said it hopefully, as though having abstained this long I might be cured and off the kick. I think he was commending my self restraint. Just this once:

Burning Leaves
There's orange and gold and scarlet on the fields,
    Beside the somber black of earth new-plowed;
A woman burning red and yellow leaves,
    The pale blue spiral twisting to a cloud.

One afternoon like this we walked alone
    Through orchards and beneath a bent old oak,
The spice of ripened apples mingling with
    The faint and stirring pungency of smoke.

No need of words to mar that perfect hour
    Which hangs star-bright against the midnight blue
Of other days. A whole eternity
    Is etched in poignant silences anew.

These many years! Again the flowing flame
    Of scarlet oak. Again the autumn sheaves.
Love, laughter, pain and parting, life and death
    Are blended in the smell of burning leaves.

—October 17, 1962

*   *   *

The mammas and maiden aunts and female family friends of young ladies were sharper in what is called the olden times.

They invented the chaperone system which made it unthinkable for a young lady to be asked out to a restaurant or theater by a young man without being accompanied by an older woman. The chaperones got squired about, got fed fancy fare, saw the good shows and were treated charmingly by pleasant young men, all at their expense.

It must have resulted in short courtships.

—November 29, 1962

*　　*　　*

Our daughter-in-law, Marilyn, still thinks it was something of a miracle that brought them a Christmas tree one year.

She wanted a tumbleweed tree, but none could be found near their home on Pierre Street in Manhattan. But one windy afternoon she went outside and there in a corner of the garage was a big round tumbleweed, blown along the highway from no telling where, into the town. A special turn of the wind had guided it into Pierre Street and another special shift into their driveway and into the trap of the garage.

Sometimes it is easier to believe in miracles than in chance.

—December 27, 1962

*　　*　　*

Going through my mother's things after her death I found photographs, letters, postcards, clippings, each tied together neatly. One box was label-ed, "String too short to save."

—January 30, 1963

A Nuisance

A nuisance that could be spared is the apologizer. She is always belittl-ing herself—most apologizers are women—her cooking, her personal ap-pearance and her state of being. All she accomplishes is to make people feel uncomfortable as they mouth hurried compliments in refutation of the apologies.

The apologizer invites you to dinner. Nothing is fit to eat—her own words, for actually the food is excellent. She mentions that the roast is overdone, or maybe underdone, the lemon pie runny, the coffee too weak or too strong.

Over and over you assure her that the food is delicious, that the coffee is exactly the specific gravity you prefer, and that you love meat with a crisp crust or red juices, whichever it is.

After dinner there is no opportunity to discuss world events or the divorce of a mutual friend. She lists the furniture piece by piece, while it stands by listening to its infirmities. The upholstery on that chair by the bookcase is wearing thin and another is faded, the ladder-back chair has a long scratch and the davenport cushions are leaning.

As to herself, whatever she has on is a candidate for the rag bag, besides which her hair is a sight. She has either just had a permanent and it has not settled down yet, or she is badly in need of one. A person never seems to catch her in between.

After several such sessions you become so annoyed you feel like agreeing with her.

—February 5, 1963

Mellow With Memories

As we moved out of the old Capital-Journal building Saturday night we gathered to cast a last, longing, lingering look behind.

The old building is mellow with memories. It has listened in on the lives of many people, listened with cheers and with tears. It holds special memories for each person who has worked there, memories that are now all mingled together in tossed nostalgia.

Charles Sessions was managing editor of the Capital when I began writing this column 30 years ago this fall. He once told me, "Remember two things—never make light of a woman's house or her husband." Scholarly Harold P. Chase was editorial writer and Tom McNeal filled in another corner with wit and gay debonair worldliness.

Milton Tabor succeeded Mr. Sessions and managed the editorial page. World War II brought paper shortages. Type grew smaller and huddled together on the page till the paper looked like a dark cloud hanging in the southwest. It was a good lesson in picking and choosing words.

The Capital editorial writer is now Gordon Martin. He grumbles about where I put commas and I don't suppose he will be any different in the new building. I hope not, for from his fund of knowledge he can fix my mistakes. George Mack is the present one of several Sunday editors I have worked with.

During these 30 years my children and my grandchildren have stood in wide-eyed awe at the big press turning out papers and at news coming and printing itself on paper, and at all the wonders of a large newspaper plant.

Saturday night the press was on its last run. A pressman said he intended to save the very last paper and give it to Oscar Stauffer. The news room was vacant, the floor littered with paper. In the composing room, linotypes were being swung out the side of the building and moved to the new plant.

The new building is beautiful and shiny, and it is beginning to store away memories. In a few years we will be asking each other, "Remember the night we moved in, how it rained, and the party?" They will begin for me when I take this column to 616 Jefferson, the first one to be set and printed in the beautiful shiny building. It will listen, too, as people work and live.

—May 7, 1963

Sound of an Epic

A person wonders what chain of events led up to the moment and that place in the Dallas street when President Kennedy, gay and happy as he waved to cheering admirers, was suddenly struck down by an assassin's bullet. His death carried on the strange coincidence that every president elected in a year divisible by 20, beginning in 1840 has died in office.

The president, in hearty good humor, made a talk interrupted by laughter and applause. Referring to the interest in women's clothes, he said, "Nobody bothers about what Lyndon and I wear."

137

At the end of the talk he was presented with a white cowman's hat and a pair of boots and Jackie was given a pair of boots. Although mildly encouraged to do so, he did not put the hat on. We have had clownish presidents, but John Kennedy was not one. Instead he said easily, "Wait till I get back to the White House Monday."

He could not know that on Monday he would be laid to rest in Arlington cemetery. Nor could any of the gay breakfasters know that within three hours he would lie dead in Parkland Hospital.

The communications system, as shown in these last days, is capable of focusing the whole world on a single event. The television stations, the radios and newspapers did a prodigious job of bringing news swiftly to the people of the tragic happenings since Friday noon.

The sound of muffled drums, of caisson wheels on brick pavement, of horses' hooves, of a bugler playing taps, of multitudes walking through the Capitol rotunda were heard by millions of people sitting in their homes. They saw the gray horses, the flag-wrapped casket, the young servicmen who came to honor their dead commander-in-chief, and the great of the world who came to honor a man they respected.

I wonder if a good many Americans have not learned more about John Kennedy in his death than they knew during his life. The words of his inaugural address as they have been repeated these last days have the sound of an epic. They deserve to be cut in stone.

Jacqueline Kennedy has won the esteem and honor of the nation, of the world. She was at first thought to be a shy young woman, but it was soon evident that she was not shy in fulfilling any duty or obligation. Her courage in doing the last things she could for her husband was superb and flawless.

She acted at all times with dignity, but not the dignity of coldness. She was not afraid to show feeling and sentiment, but feeling and sentiment simply and quietly expressed. She neither "put herself forward," nor shrank into the background.

We have had many First Ladies, women of many different kinds, each expressing her own personality, from home-loving Bess Truman to world-concerned Eleanor Roosevelt. But none, at least in recent times, have had the luster and shine of Jackie Kennedy—and be certain of this, the luster and shine go deeper than the surface.

—November 26, 1963

Preston and Anna

Preston and Anna Hale were among the first people I knew after I married and came to live on a Chase county farm. They had also just been married. He was serving as the county's first agricultural agent.

When we moved to Topeka 15 years later, the Hales also came. Preston had been hired as county agent for Shawnee. We have been close friends during these years and I have been amazed at the many ways in which he has used his skill and talent.

138

He worked toward a complete good life for farmers, mixing conservation with square dancing and encouraging youth to go to college. While park commissioner of Topeka, he made major improvements in city parks and acquired valuable new land while it could be bought. He is an excellent gardener, an expert photographer and a number one promoter, without pay, of many worthwhile projects.

He has made beautiful furniture, cut and polished stones for jewelry, and a few years ago took up oil painting and turned out some nice pictures.

The admirable thing about Preston is that he gets in motion and does things instead of just talking about them. The only time he has ever failed was when he undertook to make a jacket for Anna, in the same style as one she had which he liked.

He got material, spread it out on a big table, laid the jacket over it and cut around it. It seemed the sensible, direct thing to do, but somehow the pieces didn't go together and he had to give it up.

But it is still stored on a closet shelf and he just might do something with it one of these days.

—March 19, 1964

*   *   *

It beats all. A few weeks ago the political writers were filling columns about the New Hampshire primary. They speculated and reported and generally gave the impression that it was a major event in which the fate of the nation was involved.

But do you know what? Now that it is over, these same writers are saying it didn't amount to a hill of beans, was just a few remote New Englanders voting their local prejudices, and nobody should pay any attention to its results."

—March 20, 1964

*   *   *

The japonica and forsythia are lazy this year. The blooms come slow and scattered, like the first grains of popping corn.

—April 24, 1964

*   *   *

This is May Day and I hope you have a young neighbor to slip a May basket over your door knob. It will probably be made of a sheet of school tablet or newspaper and in it will be a few slightly wilted violets, a sprig of sweet William, one of lilac and a few dandelions curling at the edges. But the best thing is unseen - the love of a child.

—May 1, 1964

The Beatles

I have seen the phenomenon of the times, the Beatles. I say "seen" rather than "heard," because scarcely a word was audible over the screaming of young American femininity.

139

My excuse for going was to chaperone my granddaughter, Melissa Hanger, and one of her friends, Marla Wambsgans. We journeyed to Kansas City on the special train, and in our coach was Robert Sutton, College of Emporia sophomore, who provided a preview with his Beatle hair down to his eyes. Girls flocked around him and called him "George," the Beatle he was thought most to resemble. Oh yes, he washes his hair with Prell.

Tension was almost beyond endurance as the crowed waited for their idols while a thin girl with long platinum hair gyrated before the microphone. I suppose she was singing, though the sound, and responses from the audience, was more like monotonous shouting.

"Just to think," a girl breathed, "that behind that curtain are the Beatles!"

In time the curtain parted and the Beatles were bowing as a great scream tore from young throats and bulbs flashed like heat lightning. Binoculars were snatched back and forth and all the time that great piercing shriek rose and fell. The Beatles cavorted nimbly and Ringo's mop flew in unison with his drumbeat. Their movements were full of charm and grace.

"There's Paul," a girl moaned through tears. "Isn't he sweet standing there!"

It was a materialization of an intense desire. A painter would have agonized over the adoration on young faces, the exaltation, the fire and fervor, the near despair as the audience realized the program was about over. "Oh, please don't go," they groaned.

The Beatles seem nice wholesome, modest young men. The feeling they arouse is not just romantic fervor. The girls are mostly 10 to 14, a kind of at-odds age, too young to be real teenagers, but hurried too fast through their childhood by over-exposure to sophistication.

The young are capable of great feeling, strong emotion and direct action when greatly moved. Their response to the Beatles may be like the emotion aroused by a revival or that which sent thousands of young children on the tragic children's crusades.

It was an intense experience, too soon over. Instead of the pleasant satisfaction that ends good entertainment, there was a troubled air as of something unfinished.

—September 20, 1964

G-E-O-G-R-A-P-H-Y

When I was a child the first thing a pupil did when he got a new geography book was to complete a sentence, a sentence with each word beginning in turn with the letters G E O G R A P H Y, Until this was done on the title page inside the book it could hardly be called usable.

The version in Union School in Hickory County, Mo., was "George Elliot's Oldest Girl Rode A Pig Home Yesterday." What idle pupil first thought of it was never asked. It was just something that was done.

I hadn't thought about it in years, but if I had I would suppose it had long been forgotten. But a few weeks ago my grandson Jimmy in Manhattan showed me his geography, and there it was, written in with only a slight change: "George Elliot's Old Grandfather Rode A Pig Home Yesterday."

The boundaries of nations have changed, capital cities have changed, life has changed, in the colored outlines on the maps, but the old symbol remains. That first idle student must have long since disappeared down the dim corridors of the past, unsung, but not forgotten.

—January 30, 1965

The Little Cardinal

The little cardinal that has a nest in the climbing rose beside the living room window says more about single-hearted devotion than could be printed on a ream of paper.

About two weeks ago my granddaughter, Melissa, noticed a bird in the rose bush with a twig in her mouth, and said, "There's a bird building a nest." Sure enough, she was, and in a few days it was completed, neat and round and tidy, firmly planted in a criss-cross of vines and trellis, not two feet outside the window.

For two weeks she has been sitting on three fragile-looking little eggs, during which time there have have been hours of steady rain, nights of unusual chill, 100-degree heat and winds that swayed the trellis like a rocking horse.

But rain nor wind nor heat nor cold can deter her from her age-old duty of sitting on her eggs. She is there when darkness shuts the nest from sight and she is there at the start of another day.

Her faithfulness and devotion are not engendered by law or public opinion. She could abandon the eggs, fly away and nobody would go after her to charge her in court with egg desertion.

When the eggs are hatched, both the father and the mother cardinal will hustle to keep food in the gaping mouths. But if they chose not to, no feathered sheriff would return them to this address with a paper requiring child support.

They have no laws and need none. No bird tavern tempts them to leave the nest for an evening of noisy pleasure. Their pleasure is to sit on the nest quietly and bring the treasures in it to their destined culmination.

The cardinal may know, or she may not, that life is growing in the eggs beneath her. It is no matter, for something stronger than knowing or willing causes her to sit all day and all night through heat and cold and rain and wind.

I would like to praise her patience, her faithfulness, her courage, her devotion, but they are beyond praise. She is more shining than words on a piece of paper.

—September 8, 1965

141

*   *   *

Much of the world's art is concerned, particularly at Christmas, with "Mother and child—." Can we look ahead in the future, I wonder, to "Sitter and child?"

—October 16, 1965

What Emma Would Like

The tenderness of Christmas centers around Mary and the baby, but the world has too little regard for the love of Joseph, who cared so faithfully for Mary and their child.

"And he arose and took the young child and his mother" and fled with them to Egypt, to remain until the death of Herod, who had ordered that all sons born to Hebrew families should be killed.

These evenings fathers sit in crowded stores holding babies in their arms or stand patiently looking after small children while their wives shop.

One young father, with the bronzed skin of an outdoor worker, held a baby wrapped in a pink blanket, the child's soft head pillowed against his rough work jacket.

The baby slept peacefully and the father stood quietly waiting for his wife to choose between a hand mirror and a string of beads. She brought them to him to ask his advice, "Which do you think Emma would like?"

"They're both real nice," he said. Then, seeing the frustration of indecision that was engulfing her, he said, "Get the beads, mamma. They'll look pretty on her." The woman sighed with the relief of one more decision made.

Not much is said about fathers at Christmas time, but perhaps Joseph, who took the child and his mother to safety, has a special blessing for fathers who are kind and patient with children and their mothers.

—December 21, 1965

A Tornado

A tornado roared savagely through the town and is being answered by the snarl of saws and the thud of hammers. It tore across the town in minutes, but the damage will scarcely be repaired in years.

Along with the adjective "unbelievable," another is heard, "lucky." It might seem that there was little to feel lucky about in such a disaster, but it is a word used with fervent sincerity.

Those whose homes were spared feel lucky, almost with an apology to have been so fortunate when a slight veering of the awesome funnel would have razed their homes instead of some that were ruined.

People whose homes are still habitable, even with a roof off and windows boarded up, feel lucky to be able to remain in their homes and look after their possessions. And those whose homes and cars were a total loss, but who came out of the basement unharmed, say how lucky they are to be alive. Among these last were Barton and Peggy Griffith, who were also lucky enough to find an apartment to move to.

142

One thing is sure. The tornado made a believer of those who scoffed at weather warnings, who said the weather men "make a big fuss about every little wind" and that they had lived a good many years and never seen a tornado. Now when Bill Kurtis says to get to the basement, we'll get.

Bill was a real hero staying on the air and urging people so earnestly to take shelter when he must have longed to rush home and look after his wife Helen and their baby daughter.

There is little talk of anything but the tornado. We seem to have forgotten there is a war in Viet Nam, that stresses and strains are tensing other areas of the world. Most everybody has a tale of the freakish behavior of the funnel.

A bath towel was driven into a door at the Embassy apartments so firmly that a man could not pull it out.

A partition was carried away at the IBM office on Topeka Avenue, but two paper cups were left standing.

The six pillars of Mae Rohrer's porch at 1607 Mulvane were torn down and splintered, but a pot of geraniums bloomed on unharmed.

The roof was lifted off J. B. Hart's home at 1330 West 17th, but lamps and other glassware that was in the attic were untouched.

Two heavy table lamps in the Huntington apartment of Larry and Helen DiPietro were smashed to bits, while a small china dish of pins standing between them was undisturbed.

Framed photographs were tossed into the yard at 1274 Van Buren, and the glass was not broken. A side of the house came off, but an antique gilt water pitcher didn't have a chip.

A ceramic cat and a bunch of artificial flowers looked strange reposing near the rubble of a building. They had been found and rescued.

A red rocking chair stood on a lawn as though inviting the owner to sit and rest.

The windshield of a car, SN 27683, was marked with two large perfect spiderwebs. An artist couldn't have done them better.

One of the most desolate ruins left by the tornado is Central Park. It was a quiet, pleasant square of grass and trees and a little lake, no animals but squirrels and birds and other small creatures that lived there, nothing to attract crowds.

Every tree, it seems, was twisted off. Stark, jagged trunks rise from a tangle of underbrush and stand bare and denuded, a scene that calls to mind an artist's conception of a lifeless planet.

The awesome thing about the funnel was its tremendous force, which was emphasized by its swiftness. Some trees were twisted, some broken, some uprooted. Two huge trees on 15th Street west of College Hill were pulled up, bringing not only a large section of earth-bound roots, but also a whole square of concrete sidewalk. Two others just as large were uprooted with pavement in the 1300 block on West 17th.

If men undertook to dig up a giant tree, it would require many hours of work with big machines. The whirling spiral did it in a twinkling.

It was a tragic destruction of trees in the scorching sweep across the city. Estimates have been made of the number of homes and businesses destroyed, but there is no way to count the death of the trees.

If money is available, houses can rise quickly again, but the trees cannot be replaced in a generation.

Children played on fallen trees, making believe they were bridges. A small girl on West 17th spoke to me, "Your know what I got from the tornado?" I asked what it was.

"A piece of tree," she said brightly. "I'll run and get it." She proudly brought a little chip, fresh from inside a tree, as her cherished souvenir.

—June 13, 1966

Ephemeral Beauty

The most poignant beauty is beauty that is passing, moving, flowing away like a river, beauty that is fragile and perishable—the loveliness of a child, the flame of a sunset, the sweetness of a song, the magic of a moonlight night. Such beauty is intensified by a nameless and inexpressible sadness, the sadness of change and loss.

A golden autumn afternoon with leaf smoke pungent in the air, girls in sweaters lettered with their schools sauntering home, faces serene and glowing, a boy kicking leaves in the gutter, voices of children clear in the evening air.

A woman in a blue dress raking leaves, another gathering clothes off the line, looking up at a mulberry tree gold against a blue sky. Far off a jet is marking it with a white line.

Birds have lost their nesting caution. They fly close, bold in twittering clusters, to pluck seeds from bushes and grass. Flocks of tiny black wings twinkle overhead. A cardinal helps himself to the bittersweet over the doorway, a blujay harvests berries from the cedar.

A carpet of gold sprinkles the grass. Tomorrow it will be dull brown and a chill wind will whirl the dried leaves. Trees are soft rounded billows of gold and coral and crimson clouds. Tomorrow will dull the colors and strip the branches. Tomorrow is coming, nobody can stop it, tomorrow with its cold and snow and leaden sky.

But today is warm and still and bright and golden. You want to cry out for it to stay, for time to stop and keep its beauty forever. Who, though, would give a second look if the flamboyance of fall was a year-round event? It would be as unmoving as a plastic rose.

The most cherished beauty is ephemeral, beauty that is spent, lost, vanished—the flower that fades, the song that ends, the summer that dies, and life itself flowing away like a river.

Nobody can stop it. Nobody can hold it. Tomorrow it will be gone.

—November 3, 1966

Father's Day

Sunday I guested (to use a popular TV word) with the family of my son-in-law, Dick Hanger, and took him a couple of ties, which I thought were received with mixed feelings. After we had consumed the steak he broiled in the copper fireplace, he suggested we all go for a walk by the lake—Lake Shawnee.

It was deep night, with a half moon casting a pale shine over the earth. It dropped gold into the water and polished the trees. Thick leaves cast shadows as dark and deep as pools.

The night was so still that only the faintest ripples could be seen on the lake, which could have been a great polished floor. The night was so still that the world could have been cast into an enchantment.

Frogs were singing their nightly hymn of joy. It was a choir of young voices and only after they had warmed up did the bull frog add the harmony of his deep down bass.

It was a perfect June night—the poet should also have written about a night in June. We heard the night murmur and saw it glisten.

—June 21, 1967

*   *   *

With all the walk-outs, sit-downs, love-ins, take-offs and put-ons, ordinary people need to become hold-ons—hold on to common sense.

The hippies with their love-ins are more subtle than the beatniks with their tough defiance. The hippie claims to love everybody. He hands out flowers, which he probably helped himself to, and is brimming over with good will.

A policeman might be irritated when a bearded barefoot youth hands him a wilted flower and says he loves everybody, but there is no law against flowers and love. Everybody thinks well of both.

A rock-throwing gang can be handled, but what can be done with an outfit that proclaims love for one and all?

—July 7, 1967

*   *   *

Friendship is a delicate thing. Two people may be friends for years, but let one unpleasant matter come between them and the friendship is ruined. Friendship survives absence, even neglect, and can be taken up again without losing anything, but it does not survive a painful event in which one of the persons feels he has not been treated well or has not been understood.

This delicacy is also felt in the matter of reputation. A man may lead a blameless life for many years, then make one misstep that undoes all that he has built up.

A cashier in a bank may handle his employer's money for 30 years, never taking a penny, but if in the 31st year he embezzles money, that one act outweighs all his good conduct.

145

A person, speaking of him to friends, dwells on his one misstep, not on his 30 honorable years.

One drop of coloring can ruin a whole bottle of milk.

—October 3, 1967

Snow

Sunday morning I woke to the sound of shovels scraping cement and wondered if it had snowed in the night.

A look out the window gave the most stunning view of the winter, soft untouched snow on every wire, twig and roof, piled with a neat precision no hand or machine could have accomplished.

The clotheslines sagged under a load of whiteness, arched into a true geometric curve that would fit into an equation to the last flake. It had drifted softly down, a flake at a time, each clinging to the next one and merging into one shape.

Every limb except the most vertical bore its soft burden of snow, and tangled shrubs held blobs that looked like flocks of white birds. Each joining of limbs supported a triangle of white.

The ground was untouched by tracks or marks and no car had marred the smoothness of the street. It was a brief look at pristine beauty, soon to be lost by imprints of man, boy, cat, shovel and car.

True to the fleeting quality of beauty, it vanished quickly, a warm, wet snow, and no one had to be mad at it for stalling his car.

It reminded me of my father's rule for his visits—come, go before you're expected to leave and don't make a nuisance of yourself.

—February 29, 1968

Guns

Congressmen who do not want to act on gun regulation are saying we must not be hasty, must not make decisions in a panic.

Where is the haste?

It has been four and a half years since President Kennedy was shot down by a gunman and several months since Dr. Martin Luther King was shot and killed. Hundreds of others whose lives, though less known, were just as dear to them and their families, have been killed by guns.

Yet nothing was done.

Then last month Robert Kennedy was killed and reluctant congressmen said we must not act in a panic. The killing goes on, several hundred every week. Only panic is in Congress.

A good many people are against gun control. They say it will not stop the killing and that is true. But it would almost certainly do three things—limit the impulse shootings in Saturday-night family brawls, make detection of killers easier and make guns harder to obtain in the future.

Anybody who has a good character and record would not be prevented from owning a gun, but if every owner and every gun were registered, those who use guns to kill and rob would have a harder time.

The powerful gun lobby is at work on Congress. Those who would like to see more control of guns should assure their congressmen of their support. Lobbies act, because they have commercial interests.

But common ordinary citizens just talk to each other. It is time to act and let our lawmakers know we support them, if we do.

—July 9, 1968

Kansas

Rich with the mold of a million years,
Rich with courage and faith and tears.

Root and leaf and flesh and bone
Rock and ice and fire. Ancient seas
Laid down wondrous masonries;
Sea creatures left their shape in stone.

Brain and will and heart and hand —
Men who did not know retreat
Planted the prairie seas to wheat
And coaxed rich life from an untamed land.

Fair and wanton, wild and dark,
Majestic in your stormy ways,
Beloved in your gentle days —
A curve of hill, a song of meadowlark.

Drama of earth and time and man,
Of stories told and ballads sung
Of battles fought and victories won.
Never will be such a state again.

—January 25, 1969

*   *   *

My cat Goodie is a year old today. Sometimes I wonder if people are kind to animals in making them household pets, or if it is another form of selfishness and arrogant power.

Goodie knows nothing about any of her kind. She rarely sees another cat and I wonder if she remembers her mother and her three brothers. They had a wonderful time together, racing through the house, climbing over the chairs, rolling objects on the floor. They probably thought those days would never end, but the family was cruelly separated.

Now she is all alone. I have deprived her of motherhood and the society of her kind. In return all she has is good food, a comfortable place to sleep, the run of the house and the doubtful pleasure of my company.

—March 20, 1969

Skimming the Cream

*   *   *

Our son Willard has just returned from a trip to France, where he was sent by his firm, Internationl Business Machines, to confer with a business firm in Nice about a custom-built computer.

On returning he told of the fine service in his hotel at Nice, how he set out his shoes and they got shined and about the breakfast menu in his room. He could indicate his choice of food or if he saw nothing he wanted, could write in a suggestion of what he wanted to eat in his room. He wondered if this kind of service might not be obtained at home.

It might, his wife Marilyn suggested, if his write-in was grape nuts flakes.

—December 29, 1969

*   *   *

Some friends of Dick Hanger are wondering why he failed to take a dip in Lake Shawnee in November, since he favored all the other months beginning with early summer.

In the middle of December on a cold windy day as the family was eating breakfast, Dick saw something dark and moving in the west cove of the lake just across from his home. It was a puppy struggling in the icy water.

Dick hurried to the cove, broke the ice and waded out waist-deep to rescue the little dog. It had started to cross the cove on ice and the ice had broken.

It was shivering and so nearly exhausted it almost collapsed, but, wrapped in a warm blanket and fed, it soon recovered. The Hangers were unable to learn who the owners were, but when the dog was turned loose later in the day it finally went off, presumably to its home, although it showed a strong inclination to linger where it had found such good friends.

—December 29, 1969

148

*"Arsenic and Old Lace" at Washburn University Theatre with Mabel Remmers and
k Prouty - 1974.*

th cast of "Mary White", and ABC television movie - 1977.

Playwright William Gibson returns for reunion at Topeka Civic Theatre - 1974.

As Vita Louise Simmon in Topeka Civic Theatr "Harvey" - 1976.

In long running melodrama "Love Rides the Rails" - villian Bill Bishop.

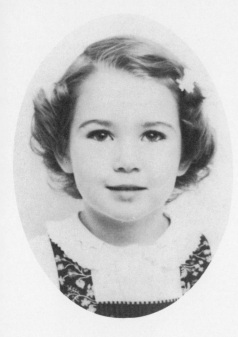

My grandchildren - Joyce and Jim Greene (above), David and Melissa Hanger.

Reading the paper with Fancy. Joyce (above) with Goodie.

Vacation in Florida with Dick and Dorothy on their boat the Ying Yang.

Great grandchildren - Matt and April Stevens, (above); Adrianne Greene, (below right). Neighbors Sue Holm and sons, Andrew and Eric McHenry.

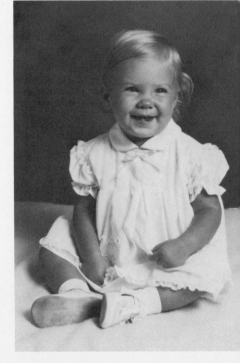

ith Senator Nancy Landon Kassebaum - 1983.

t home - my office in background.

The family, October 31, 1983. At right in the two top rows are my son Willard and his wife Marilyn. Next are their son Jim, and his wife Barbara and their daughter Adrianne. Left are their daughter Joyce, her husband Dennis Stevens and below, their children, April and Matt. At right below are my daughter Dorothy, her husband, Richard Hanger and between them their son David. Above are their daughter Melissa and her husband Ken LaZebnik. I am by Melissa.

V
1970-1983

It Was Business

In earlier years idealistic young people wanted to be missionaries and save the souls of the benighted heathen.

Now the idealistic young want to go into the Peace Corps or into social work or into some other field of personal service—all supported by money from outside sources.

These young people probably regard business as a dullish undertaking suited to the materialistic mind, an occupation for those interested in money-making, but one that offers no challenge to the intellectual.

Yet missionaries and social workers and all similar endeavors, including the ministry and teaching, are supported by the people who make money, those engaged in business and the professions. Money for these efforts comes from the government, from local taxing units, from donations by individuals and from foundations set up by business.

No personal service kind of work could be carried on if it were not for the crowds of people who go to work every day in the market places and create the wealth that supports those who have passion to serve mankind.

This is by no means an intention to downgrade these valuable services or the good people who perform them. It is only a wish to voice appreciation for those who make it possible. It is the fruit that was tended and nurtured by business.

In the earliest time it was an effort just to stay alive. All work went toward the bare necessities of finding enough food to eat and providing clothes and a shelter from the cold.

People began to find better ways of doing things, of growing food, of preserving it through a winter of weaving and building. In time there were inventions and discoveries of power and transportation and communications and all the things that make our lives interesting and comfortable.

These things came from the work of people who wanted to make money. They made it possible for artists to work at their art, for learning and education and for the development of the many social services.

But it was not the work of dull minds. It was imaginative and creative work. It was business.

—June 24, 1970

Fourth of July Picnic

Observing preparations being made by my daughter and son-in-law, Dick and Dorothy Hanger, for a picnic at Lake Perry, I was struck with the difference between then and now.

In earlier days, a family would fry two chickens, make potato salad and baked beans, along with pickles, pie, cake and lemonade. The lemonade in the vacuum jug would be the only cool food. Everything else took on the temperature of the day, usually warm.

For our Sunday expedition to see the sailboat races, the charcoal grill was loaded on the big boat, to be trailed behind the car. Steaks were taken, frozen; corn, partially cooked, buttered and rolled in foil; vegetable salad was made; grapes, cherries, cheese, crackers, doughnuts and cinnamon buns were taken for snacking on the boat. All the food was packed with ice in insulated chests.

In the evening Dick set the grill on the back of the boat, cooked the steaks, finished the corn, and we enjoyed a delicious hot and cold dinner, just as we would at home. The only item the same in then and now picnics was the fruit punch in the vacuum jug.

Those in the races ate in a big tent at the top of a long stairway through the trees, which, in the mystery of moonlight, looked as though it should lead to a temple. A good many families were camped in their own tents.

Grandchildren Melissa and Jim were the crew for Bob Douglas in the races. The top excitement was when Melissa, the lightest, was hoisted in a "bosun's chair" to the top of Bob's mast to attach a weathervane. The long, double line of masts, dark against the evening sky, were off the perpendicular, making the sky seem to lean.

After dinner and a few fireworks, Dick took us on a moonlight ride to the far end of the big lake. There was only the misty moon and the far lights along the shores, with no other boat in that wide darkness but a ghostly sailboat, not seeming to move.

Moonlight and water—how gloriously they blend their enchantments. It was not moonlight making a path on still water, but moonlight on water that looked like fresh-plowed ground and the glisten was like a soft fresh snowfall, with the boat making a dark road, splashing spray on each side like shoveled snow.

Soon the spell took over and there was no thought in the mind, only the water and the moonlight, the boat's sound and movement and the spray. I marveled that in that expanse of dark water the skipper found his way unerringly.

—July 7, 1971

Hot Pants

Girls in one of the state offices want to wear hot pants to work, but the boss says no.

I can not concur with the plea of the girls that their reason for wishing to wear hot pants is to be cooler. It is the reason given, but not, I believe, the true one.

With skirts as short as they are — and some are as short as shorts — the young ladies could not be cooler wearing the desired pants. It is a question whether they would even be as cool, with the pants heavier and tighter around the legs compared to the skirts fluttering free. This is to assume that the same brief undergarment would be worn with both.

The young ladies are motivated, I suggest, not so much by a wish to be cool as a wish to be mod. When did comfort ever enter into the style picture?

Girls who are wearing boots this July, and I have seen a number being worn, are not wearing them to keep warm. You can be sure of that. Nor are the ones who are wearing long dresses in the daytime doing so to add warmth to the lower limbs. Likewise, the heavy belts buckled about waists are adding warmth and weight, but the main thing is that they are adding style.

Comfort is of little concern to women until their later years. Ladies have laced themselves into tight corsets, popped heavy hats on their heads, pushed their feet into shoes that pinched their toes and tilted them forward, encased their necks in collars that almost closed the air passage, worn half a dozen petticoats under skirts that trailed in the dust.

They have modified their appearance with bustles and padded bras, wigs, falls, false eyelashes. They have had their faces lifted and their eyebrows tweezed.

None of these things was done for comfort. The burden of these excesses was borne because it was the stylish thing to do or in the hope of improving their appearance. This summer the style is hot pants.

Let it be said that women are willing to suffer, if need be, to improve their appearance or to keep in style. Whether they do so to impress other women or to attract the attention of men is a matter of opinion. Perhaps for both reasons.

—July 23, 1971

159

Apollo 13

There is still a tingling thrill at the blast-off of a moon rocket, the kind of teary, throat-choking feeling of the flag going past at the head of a band. You know that inside the slender rocket three men are being hurled away from the earth at a tremendous speed into the darkness of outerspace and eventually to the moon.

The earthmen watched, through a miracle of communication, two men walking on the moon, heard their voices coming through 240,000 miles of space. That seems a feat as marvelous as the means by which the men reached the moon. The whole thing is fantastic, unbelievable as we view that lovely orb from the earth palely cool and remote.

As the men filled their sacks with rocks I thought of that third man, orbiting the moon all alone for three days. Every time something was reported not to be working quite right, I was uneasy. There was no highway patrol to come along and fix it. But there was NASA in Houston, noting every minute detail and giving directions across the dark space.

They brought the crippled Apollo 13 home safely and I am confident their eye was on the Falcon.

This restless half of the 20th century may not be the best time in which to live, but I am glad to be alive at that giant step of mankind—when man first set foot on another heavenly body.

—August 5, 1971

A Commendable Trait

The many welfare problems reminded me the other day of a poor family in a small town that worried and exasperated the members of a church. It was before the government began caring for the needy and the church took the family as its special project.

The father was good-natured and shiftless. The mother took things easy. The grandparents were convinced that the Lord would provide. These, with a constantly increasing number of children, made up a family that could be called light-hearted, and light-heartedness can be a commendable trait.

An elder in the church gave the poor folks a couple of shoats for their winter's meat and felt the glow that comes from doing a good deed.

The porkers were lovingly tended and stuffed with whatever was left from the table until they grew in stature and weight. Then one day the family drove them to town and traded the pigs for a used car.

Sternly reprimanded, the man admitted that maybe it would have been better to have killed them for meat, but the children got so attached to the cute things they couldn't bear to see them killed, and anyway, mamma had been poorly and not able to get out much.

When he shrewdly added that maybe now they'd be able to get to church, there was little the good elder could say.

160

Another time a neighbor gave the family a hen and chickens to start them in poultry raising. When the chickens reached the broiler stage they were sold to make the down payment on a radio.

Confronted by the indignant donor, the man said his wife's father, who was crippled up with rheumatism, couldn't get to church and he loved to hear the sermons on the radio. He added piously that the Lord had always provided for them and he guessed He always would.

At Christmas time the Ladies Aid took up a collection and gave it to the mother to buy food for their dinner. The excited shoppers came home with 10 pounds of assorted colored candy, five pounds of nuts and ropes of glittering tinsel to hang over the torn wallpaper. Mamma had thought the tinsel would brighten up the house and make a cheerful Christmas.

The good church people were without an answer when the man quoted the scripture about taking no thought for the morrow and about the sparrows in the field. They could do nothing but stutter and stammer, for was not this man putting their own doctrine into practical application?

—September 15, 1971

Fair Trial

A letter has been received marked "Urgent Message," though it was mailed at bulk rate. It was an appeal for money by Angela Davis to help in her defense at her forthcoming trial, though one begins to wonder if the trial will ever take place.

I somehow sense a planned scheme in the repeated assertions that Miss Davis will not receive a fair trail, as though it might be based on the premise that if a thing is repeated often enough it is believed.

It is true that justice has sometimes been anything but just and perhaps the black have been victims more often than the white, though they certainly have not been the only ones. I think it is also true that there are people who will move the balance in favor of the black, mindful of the injustices they have been dealt in so many ways.

"In the final analysis," Miss Davis said in the letter, "it is not so much I who am on trial as America," referring to her coming trial as "what may be a legal lynching." She brings up Sacco and Vanzetti, saying, "If all those who want to end what Bartolomeo Vanzetti called the days 'when man is wolf to man' will treat this case as theirs, a democratic victory is possible."

This seems a bit far afield. Rather than protesting her innocence, she is making an emotional appeal in several directions.

She thinks that bail has been unjustly denied her. The reason may be because she disappeared immediately after the crime and fled from authorities. I do not know.

She said an investigator hired to examine her cell found a two-way intercom capable of picking up conversations between her and her lawyers.

Why a two-way? If the place was bugged by authorities they would not likely expect to communicate with her. Whatever the circumstances, the truth should come out.

I am among the many, and I feel sure there are many, who hope for a just and fair trial for Angela Davis, and undoubtedly there will be those involved who will challenge any show of injustice. The circumstances will tend to make everybody extremely careful.

I do not know any reason why Angela Davis will not receive a fair trial and I am becoming a little wary of continued assertions to the contrary. They are beginning to show an earmark.

—December 4, 1971

To A Little Girl

Some years ago I wrote a poem in my column "To a Little Girl on Her First Birthday." Today I am saying Happy Birthday to that girl. In the poem I said:

For a whole year
We have watched you grow
From a tiny atom of life
To a big girl
Who can take a few wobbly steps,
Reaching out for a guiding hand.
So soon
You will have to walk alone
With no one to cling to
When the going is rough.
And, little girl,
I am grieved for you to learn
How very little
Big folks know
About the going, anyway.

—December 14, 1971

Heroes

If Kansas has a single renowned hero it would be John Brown, though he had been labeled with some extreme anti-hero names. But heroes always are.

New information about Brown came from a visitor in Topeka, Mrs. James Holm, of Kent, Ohio. She was one of three who in 1969 wrote a history of their church for its 150th anniversary. It began as a Presbyterian church, became Congregational and is now the First United Church of Christ.

John Brown, who was living in Franklin Mills, joined the church Feb. 15, 1838. His wife Mary and three sons, John Jr., Jason and Owen, joined the church March 4 of the same year. Brown's actions to free the slaves were beginning during those years and he became immediately known, on joining the church, as a strong anti-slavery man. Franklin Mills was the early name of the town that is now Kent.

Against the wishes of the minister, Stephen W. Burritt, and a deacon, Elisha Beach, and against their strong admonitions, Brown brought the blacks who attended services, up front and seated them in his family pew.

They had been given seats by themselves where the stove stood, near the door, which was not a good place, Brown said, for seeing the minister and the singers, and not a true view of Christianity.

Some of the citizens and church members were friendly to Brown. Others saw him as a fanatic. Some men of influence and wealth helped finance his plan to root out slavery. When he was hanged on Dec. 2, 1859, the church bells in Kent tolled for an hour.

For a renowned Kansan of this century, I name Alfred M. Landon. No fanatic is he, no zealot betting his life for a cause, no crusader dying for that cause.

Since the time he ran for President of the United States and lost, as any Republican would have in that year of 1936, his townsmen, his fellow Kansans and his countrymen have seen him grow in character and distinction.

No anger, bitterness or sullenness were shown when he carried only two states. Instead, his humor, tolerance and maturity caught the attention of the public. Through the years he has grown in wisdom and judgment, grown past political partisanship, and many journey to Topeka to talk with him and seek his opinions, which are thoughtful and considered.

A respected, admired, beloved Kansan of this century—Alf Landon.

—January 29, 1972

*   *   *

A little girl who wanted her father to make her a swing used the same argument her mother uses to get the grass cut: "I'm ashamed for children to come here when I don't have anything to play with."

—July 10, 1972

*   *   *

November is the menopause month—now hot, now cold, gloom overhead and settling down into a gray chill. What happened to a sky that was once so blue and sunny?

A breath of summer lingers—grass is green, a flower bravely holds on, a few golden leaves quiver on the trees. But where is the warmth, the joyousness that sent the blood racing?

Nor has winter yet arrived. But it is on the way and has sent word of its coming. There is no singing. The birds have gone, leaves rattle across the ground, nothing ahead but chill winds and winter cold.

But there is a hormone for November—a wood fire burning and flaming with the sensual pleasure of sight and sound and scent and feel against the gloom of summer's ending.

—November 17, 1972

Thanksgiving

It was a perfect day, Thanksgiving at the home of my daughter and son-in-law Dick and Dorothy Hanger. Their son David, a KU senior, was there. Melissa, a sophomore at Macalester College in St. Paul, phoned.

Thirteen sat down to dinner, but no bad luck was involved since they sat at two tables. They included members of the family in both directions, all the branches and twigs — Mr. and Mrs. C. R. Van Nice — Mrs. Van Nice is Dick's mother — and Harlan and Thea Van Nice of Lawrence and their children, John and Joan — John is being married in January — and Thea's mother, Mrs. Dora Scott.

New twigs were my granddaughter Joyce and her husband, Lt. Dennis Stevens, who came from Wichita Falls, Tex. Dennis will be stationed at Forbes Air Force Base.

The weather was perfect, the Nebraska-Oklahoma game stunning and the dinner abundant and delicious, beginning with goose and turkey and ending with pumpkin and cherry pie. Everybody stayed for supper and everybody took some food home.

Three loads of dishes were washed, pool was played, the papers were read and eight or nine of the company engaged in a game called bridge, but nobody could understand why they went down so often on low bids.

It was a day for which I am thankful, humbly so, mindful of many who were lonely and hungry.

—November 27, 1972

* * *

My niece in Missouri, Mabel Parker, writes that they can't get their pickup near the house. They have to leave it on the road and walk in and out. Cows are knee-deep and not in clover.

—February 8, 1973

At Your Homecoming

Beautiful on the mountain are the feet of those who bring good tidings.

And beautiful in the newspaper is the name of your own prisoner of war.

Through the slow weary years when even hope seemed gone, the men and their families held on and now they are about to be together again.

Nobody outside the prisoners' families can know the agony of the long waiting, marked by few letters or none at all, so that you had to wonder if he was still living, if he was dejected or if his mind held hopefully on the future.

You hardly dared think of the treatment he might be receiving, but tried to forget everything and pray that his spirit would not be broken.

And the men dragging through the slow hours—what was in their minds? Did they think of their children growing up without them, some of them children they had never seen. How did the children look, what did they think?

Would things be the same between him and his wife as when they parted? Would he be welcomed home? What would their meeting be?

It must have been bitter to see their years being wasted. But now they are coming home and each meeting will be different, personal and private. But the nation can be thankful for their home-coming.

Some of the men who have returned spoke of the sheer sensual pleasure of sunlight, of colors, the landscape, seeing people going about the business of living. Being out in the world again, seeing and hearing and smelling and touching must be something like being blind and regaining one's sight.

Helping your man catch up on the world's, the community's and the family's happenings should be an exciting and pleasant experience — Yes, boys are wearing their hair long now and yes, girls are wearing their dresses short and women are wearing pant suits. He will need to be caught up on Women's Lib and the permissiveness of movies.

He will discover that men are wearing polyester double-knit suits and knit shirts and that very little ironing is done any more, that sheets are wild colors and prices are high.

Go back five years, seven, eight and think of all the changes that have come in those years, then wonder how it would feel to have them all burst on you at your home-coming.

—February 16, 1973

* * *

When Jerry Holley was in high school and had a short crew cut, his father said, "You've got nice hair. Why don't you let it grow out?"

A few years passed and Jerry did let his hair grow out, not quite long enough to be tied with a ribbon, but an attractive neck length. His father had another comment: "Why don't you cut your hair? You look like one of those hippies."

—April 4, 1973

Uncommon Man

I remember something that the Rev. Paul Bockoven, a former Topeka minister, said: "What Christ's enemies did to him is as nothing compared to what his friends do."

The minute a nation goes to war, he said, they dress Christ up in their uniform and put him at the head of their armies. "Me und Gott" is the motto of the militarists. Every war is a just and holy war and God is on our side. We pray to him to help us destroy the enemy, and the enemy prays for help in destroying us.

But at the same time the pacifists claim him. The gentle Jesus, they declare, would not fight and kill. He was full of compassion and mercy, urged his followers to turn the other cheek, to forgive 70 times seven.

If we are capitalists we want God to bless the stock market and we raise our voices in that convenient passage, "Render unto Caesar." If we are laborers we dwell upon his trade as a carpenter and slip a union card in his pocket.

He was claimed by both sides of the slavery question. He has been quoted to support the right of kings to rule and the right to overthrow kings.

Potentates of both church and state have threatened, and do threaten, the simple people with his power to keep them under submission. Wars and bloodshed, cruelty, persecution and bigotry have been inflicted in his name. Popes in the middle ages made kings tremble with their domination.

It has been said that Christ was not militarized until about the second century. His early followers were humble people of no prominence or ambition. But as Christians gained political power they put Christ in their armies and banks and engraved his name on their money.

The new young Jesus people have a more vivid picture — the protester, the anti-establishement, independent individualist, Jesus Christ superstar — in short. All see themselves in Jesus, that mysterious, magnificent uncommon man.

—April 23, 1973

* * *

Charles L. Marshall has reached that mellow philosophic state in which small pleasures are appreciated. In his current bulletin he says, "Always pleasant to be the first one to initiate a new bar of soap."

—July 19, 1973

A Beau

The little girl who likes to hear about the olden times asked "Grandma, what was a beau like?"

"A beau," she said, smiling fondly, "was a young man who paid attention to a young lady he liked. He called at her home Sunday afternoons, riding a horse or driving a buggy and wearing his Sunday suit. They sat in the parlor, which was not used any other time except when there was a funeral or important company."

"Did they play records?"

"Oh, no, it was before the talking machines. They looked at the family album and sometimes the girl played the organ and they sang."

"Didn't they ever go on Coke dates or things like that?"

"We didn't know anything about Cokes. In the summer the girl would make a pitcher of lemonade and sometimes a plate of cookies to serve the young man. She liked to let him know she could cook."

"That sounds like dullsville. Didn't they ever have any fun?"

"Oh yes, they had fun. They both looked ahead all week to Sunday. Sometimes they held hands — the parlor was usually dark with the blinds drawn down under the lace curtains. And I guess they talked about what they were both thinking."

"What was that?"

"Getting married. He spoke to her father and asked his permission and then they were engaged."

166

"Did beaus ever bring presents?"

"Not often. We didn't have any florists, but he would bring peppermint and lemon and horehound stick candy in a striped sack and after they were engaged maybe a comb and brush and mirror set. One young man gave his girl a hope chest."

"What's a hope chest?"

"It was a cedar chest where a girl kept linens she embroidered and collected for her house—pillow cases and dresser scarves and tea towels and such things. Every girl expected to marry and looked ahead to having nice things."

"Did they ever live together first to see if they liked each other?"

"It's past your bed time. You're too young for such talk."

—September 21, 1973

One-Year-Old

It was a mild, pleasant day with a faint breeze coming in through the open door. The carpenter and his wife lingered over their morning meal, the baby in his mother's lap.

"Do you remember, Joseph," she said, "what day this is? It was a year ago that our boy was born."

He remembered and they spoke of the tedious journey and of the crowd and confusion at the inn. "I was afraid for you, Mary, and I don't know what we would have done if it had been a troubled birth."

"I was afraid too, at first, but what happened was so wonderful, that woman we didn't know coming to help me. And that bright star — was there really a bright star that came and stood over Bethlehem?"

"The brightest star I ever saw. The people came out of the inn to look at it, but none of them knew much about stars. They said they'd never seen one like it."

"I remember," mused Mary, "and it seemed like I heard people singing from far off. I must have been dreaming. . . Joseph, do you think we could have a star tonight, to remind us of that other star. Could you make a star, Joseph?"

"I could cut one out of wood. We will draw it on that little piece of board we brought from the stable, to make a bed to carry Jesus. You put your shawl over it."

Joseph cut out the little star, smoothed the edges and brought it to Mary, who went to the chest and took out a scrap of gold cloth to cover it. It caught the eye of the boy, who reached for it, took an uncertain step, then another and two more, and reached the hand his mother held out to him.

"Look, Joseph, he walked! This is his first step!"

Joseph and Mary sat down on the floor facing each other. She handed him the star and his son walked toward him, reaching for it. He caught the child tight in his arms, and Mary took the star. The boy, more sure of his steps now, walked to her and was gathered up in her arms.

167

Where, they wondered, would they put the star. They looked about and saw the new little olive tree.

"We'll put it in the top of the tree," Mary said, "and it can shine down on us the way it did in Bethlehem."

—December 24, 1973

Lynn

Lynn Martin, a friend of many years, died Nov. 1, a man made in his own mold. Most of his life was lived in the big sandstone family home in Brookville, built in 1879. He planted and tended a little grove of trees and with a scythe cut weeds and grass wherever they needed cutting and looked after the little park.

Talent and skills he had in abundance. He took photographs of the countryside and of people — lined old faces and fresh young faces — and recorded all with a poetic realism. He published a newspaper in Brookville, The Echo, and later turned it into a little magazine. They reflected the life and history of the community.

In memory of his sister, a noted high school teacher, he started a library of some 3,000 books, which he sent to anybody who wanted them, the only expenses being the return postage. No records were kept.

He wrote poetry, about thought, not things, poetry with deep quiet feeling. He made pottery, played tennis. One interest followed another or overlapped and he took each new one up with enthusiasm and his own special competence.

He had a beard before beards were in and was a dozen years ahead of the easy, relaxed Joseph's-coat styles, only his styles were his own. Summers he wore shorts, an unbottoned shirt and sandals with a white nylon cap, homemade.

He gathered wild plums and made his own jelly, marking each glass with the place the fruit was found. Dear to him was a clump of wild apple trees and every spring he went to the remote pasture to revel in the blossoms. He did his own cooking, but mostly he lived on cigarettes, which he rolled himself, and black coffee, many cups a day.

He liked little towns and country newspapers and he knew all the little towns nearby, sat and talked to the people. He loved the southwest. Once in a small town in New Mexico he gathered up the discarded Christmas trees and in the night set them in a hillside by the town, surprising the people with a grove of firs.

He visited friends, traveled to many places, and once drove his Volkswagon slowly down Fifth Avenue, New York, in his grey beard and his bright clothes, practically paralyzing New York's finest.

He was impatient and angry with trivia, pompousness, pretense. His rule was never to attend any meeting that required tight clothes. His friends knew him as different, frank, often brusque, but honest, and he gave them encouragement to be themselves, gave then a glimpse into that rare and lonely land.

Wit and sharp intelligence were his. He took a picture of steers gathered at a fence, looking ahead with mild interest and labeled it "Art Jury."

He read endlessly and enormously all his life and with a reading glass when his eyesight dimmed, and he was touched by great majestic music. Hearing Tchaikovsky's Fifth Symphony, he said, "That is the story of my life." His deep sadness was rarely revealed, but he protested vigorously up to the end of his life against stupidity and foolishness.

Some years ago he asked his son Hugh to write a few special friends after his death and to include these lines:

Say to hill and flower and tree,
"He is you and you are he"

—December 27, 1973

The Warehouse

I wish I had been there to see the piano going into the hole. The "hole" is the orchestra pit which has been cut into the floor at the Topeka Civic Theatre's new place at 534½ North Kansas Ave.

The piano was set on a big piece of plywood and eased down, with four strong men able to catch it.

Sunday afternoon the musicians were down there, some of them literally sitting under the front of the stage, which is on the floor, with seats rising in tiers. P.K. Worley, music director and also president of Civic Theatre, was taking the orchestra through "Luck, Be a Lady Tonight," one of the group's songs from "Guys and Dolls," which is being readied for the grand opening Friday night.

Families were there, children were playing, people were painting, sweeping, nailing, carrying and saying to each other, "Isn't this great!" Dancers were dancing—the chorus has some cuties—and Bill Meikle was directing.

It all added up to the pleasure of having your own place. People stood and gazed admiringly at the facilities in the rest rooms, shining new plumbing — two rooms in the lobby for the public and two upstairs in the dressing rooms for the actors. It was a goal attained — get the plumbing in. A lot of goals are still ahead.

A member of the cast, Bonnie Parton, has reason to feel sentimental about the show. It was in the cast of "Guys and Dolls" which the Civic Theatre gave a dozen years ago that she and her husband, Dick, met. She was Adelaide and he was Big Julie.

Besides opening a new theater the Civic Theatre is opening dinner theater, which will be Fridays and Saturdays for four week ends, closing Feb. 16. Regular theater is on Thursdays and a matinee on Feb. 10. The Civic Theatre number is 357-1192.

And after the weekend there will be red carpet in the theater, real carpet, but the other kind of red carpet is always out.

—January 24, 1974

Camisole

A fashion note said that a new frilly undergarment for spring was modeled on the camisole, but to a person who has seen and worn camisoles the garment illustrated has little in common.

Here is a layer-by-layer description of what in earlier days went on ahead of the dress.

First of all, a woman pulled on what was called a vest, which was like a man's sleeveless knit undershirt. Over that vest went the corset. Nobody would think of getting dressed without a corset, laced down the back and hooked in front.

The next garment was optional, the corset cover, a plain fitted muslin garment intended to give a smoother flow by softening the meeting of corset and vest.

Next came the camisole, either over the corset or the corset cover. The camisole was really the ornamental top of what later combined with petticoats to become the slip. It was made of white muslin, usually of a good quality buttoned down the front and gathered into a band at the waist.

Some were made of very wide embroidery, with the scallops at the top. Others were decorated with lace insertions and lace at the top. A really fancy camisole was made by drawing bands of thread about an inch or an inch and a half wide and fitting it with hand-made drawnwork.

Straps were made of insertion or ribbon. If of ribbon, the ribbon was run through a beading at the top of the camisole and when the armhole was reached, it looped over to the back to form a shoulder strap, continued on to the other armhole and on to the front, where ends were left to tie a bow.

The corset has supporters to hold up stockings, usually a fine cotton called lisle. Over the corset went drawers, with embroidery at the bottom, and petticoats. The number depended on the dress or skirt. A thin dress required at least three, one or two plain ones and a fancy embroidery-trimmed flounced one.

The idea was not to appear to be a biped.

—March 30, 1974

Little Things

Rich people have fewer ways of showing affection for each other than those who are poorer.

The wife of a poor man can cook his food the way he likes it. The woman with servants and housekeepers and cooks can only say, "I'm sorry, dear, but that's the way Andre cooks eggs and you know how hard it was for us to get him. But I'll speak to him."

The wife of a poor man can iron his shirts the way he likes them, trim his toenails and wash his back. The rich man's valet does these things for him.

The man in modest circumstances can show his affection and appreciation of his wife by helping with the dishes when she has had a tiring day or is not feeling well, by looking after the children at such times and by bring-

170

ing home some unexpected luxury of fruit or a roast she would have thought they could not afford.

The rich woman needs no help with her work because she doesn't have any work of that kind. The rich can buy each other expensive presents, in a situation where a diamond would entail no financial sacrifice.

There are many little things poorer people can do for each other, by their work or small amounts of money, that would have no meaning if they were rich.

Now aren't you glad you're not rich?

—July 22, 1974

A Resignation

It was an historic moment—Richard Nixon stepping down from his high office of President of the United States and turning it over to his vice president.

This first resignation of a president was preserved for the future in sound and color. Years from now the films can be run and people can see the tense face, hear the voice, near breaking sometimes with emotion.

It would be something like our being able to hear young Thomas Jefferson reading his draft of the Declaration of Independence or Washington taking charge of the Continental Army.

It may be the best speech that Mr. Nixon has ever made. He expressed no bitterness or hate, only hopes for the good of the nation. By stepping down he has relieved the Congress and the people of the agonies of Watergate.

Millions heard that historic address, wherever they were. Everything stopped while they listened. People will remember where they were, just as they remember where they were when they heard of the bombing of Pearl Harbor.

I was at a dinner theater at the Topeka Civic Theatre warehouse. A few minutes before eight o'clock, between the dinner and the show, President P.K. Worley went before the audience and said a television had been brought to the lobby and invited the people to listen. So in perfect silence we heard the President giving up his office.

It was also a sad moment in history—a president standing for the last time, as president, in the historic East Room of the White House, a room that had been so much of his life, saying au revoir, as he put it, to his staff, cabinet and friends.

He spoke of his early life, his parents, and lingered over his last farewell, then walked out of the White House for the last time as President and was flown away, for the last time, in Air Force One. His family stood by, smiling bravely.

Final goodbyes, a door closing for the last time, are painful.

Richard Nixon has stood at the pinnacle of power and success, the most important official in the world. He has been acclaimed by the peoples of China and the Soviet Republics, by Arabs, Israelites and Europeans. He

171

has widened the cooperation of the world, encouraged friendships and, one hopes, narrowed chances of war.

He won election by the largest majority ever given a President. What the future may hold for him is not known.

—August 12, 1974

Mr. Benny

Jack Benny was the greatest of them all. His long career of 65 years moved smoothly to the top and stayed. Never with him was the joke that didn't quite come off, the awkward pause, the unsure timing. He was the master with the deft touch.

He was always a pure delight, and his programs came to an end too soon. Perhaps others felt as I did, that he seemed particularly to belong to me, that he was my kind of comedian. That was part of his magic.

Jack Benny did not reach his great heights by pushing other actors down. He took them along and they shared his success—his wife Mary, Dennis Day, Phil Harris, Don Wilson, "Rochester," — and we looked ahead to hearing them each week on radio, then seeing them on television. We loved his old Maxwell, his stage stinginess, his ageless 39 years.

In comedy the line between going over and falling flat is so thin that it may hang on the way a word is said, the look on a face, the timing. Jack had the feeling for what was right and an audience was never worried for him.

If all his efforts had been directed to his violin, he would probably have become a great musician, but the world would have lost the Benny it knew and loved. He would have been another violinist with a difficult name.

When he walked out on the stage with that swing, thousands waited expectantly, knowing his first words would be a surprise. There were no uproarious jokes on his show, no smart wisecracks, no sly off-color innuendoes. His humor was original, his wit subtle. He was a kind and lovable man who had no jealousy for fellow actors, only help and appreciation. Everybody was happy to call him friend.

He was sure and confident. He needed no psychiatrist or guru. And not for him were the divorce courts, drugs and scandals. He was a great human being, a superb comedian who brought much pleasure to the world and he was first of all himself.

He was the greatest of them all and we never shall look upon his like again.

One who mourns him is a Topeka girl who hoped to see him. On one of his visits here she waited on the fringe of the crowd, then spoke to him shyly, saying how happy she was to meet him. She added that it was her birthday and seeing him was her best present.

"How old are you, dear?" he asked.

She said she was sixteen.

He kissed her and she fairly floated out of the tent.

—January 2, 1975

* * *

After having dinner with the McHenry family I announced that I must go home. At the door we stood talking. In a lull, Eric, three, asked sweetly, "Why doesn't Peggy go home? She said she was going."

—February 8, 1975

Lincoln and Two Women

Two women helped shape the life of Abraham Lincoln. Nancy Hanks Lincoln gave him birth and it may be that she gave him his dreams. Sarah Bush Lincoln gave him a mother's love.

Nancy was the daughter of Lucy Hanks, who, five years after her baby was born, without marriage, was brought into court as a loose woman. Lucy was a strong, strange girl with a "streak of flame" in her. Later she married and became the mother of eight other children.

Nancy did not live with her mother, but with her Aunt Betsy Sparrow. As a child she must have heard whisperings about her mother and felt herself different from other children.

Tom Lincoln married this dreamy, wistful, lonely girl and Nancy bore a son in their harsh little cabin set among wild crabapples. They were not blooming that Sunday the 12th of February when Aunt Betsy came to wash the new baby and put a yellow petticoat on him. But in the springs to come Nancy must have walked with her son in the quiet where dreams and hopes are root and bud with the earth.

When the boy was nine he whittled pegs for his mother's coffin, which his father made from fresh-cut pine, and they buried her in a clearing near the cabin. She was 36 years old.

Some time later his father went away on a trip and came back driving four horses to a wagon. Out of the wagon came featherbeds and pillows, a walnut bureau, chest, table and chairs, pots and pans, knives, forks and spoons. And Sarah Bush Lincoln, his father's new wife, with her three children.

Sarah was big and strong and loving. She pressed the boy's face against her and love was born between them.

That night she threw out the corn husks he had been sleeping on and he lay down on soft feathers. A hurt and lonely little boy had found a new mother.

Tom Lincoln was never one to set the world on fire, but Sarah got things done and for the first time the boy had a comfortable home and was encouraged to do and learn.

—February 12, 1975

Valentine Exchange

Yesterday we wrote about a talk Catherine Hathaway made about Valentine's Day. Among the many other things she collects and does, she has a collection of valentines.

She doesn't think the valentine exchange at schools is nearly as exciting

173

as it used to be, now that every child is expected to give a valentine to every other child in his or her room. Feelings must not be hurt.

The child comes home and says, "Mom, I gotta have valentines for Friday," and mom asks, "How many kids in your class?" He says there are 28, so mom goes out and buys the large economy size, the school pack of 30, unisex in their greetings and sentiment.

Everyone gives and everyone gets and it doesn't mean a thing, Catherine said, and added, "The whole bunch goes into the trash can on Saturday." There are no hurt feelings, and no excitement either.

"But back in those pre-psychology days," she said, "no one bothered much about delicate feelings. We may not have known anything about sex, but we knew the facts of life.

"We knew that the little girls with the big blue eyes and the naturally curly hair were going to get a lot of valentines and that the plain Janes with the pigtails were going to get just a few.

"But those few really meant something, even if they were from girl friends. If someone thought enough of you to spend a nickel or take the trouble to make you a valentine, they must like you. It was an exciting day.

"Watching Cupid's messenger make many trips to the desks of the pretty little curly-headed girls was good realistic training for life in the real world. I don't believe our psyches were too bent out of shape. The plain Janes accepted the events of valentine exchanges as just the way things were."

Happy Valentine's Day to all of you, curly heads and plain Janes alike.
—February 14, 1975

Press Conference

One of the questions asked President Ford at his press conference here was about the propriety of his having conferred with John Connally in Texas, since Connally has been indicted.

The President defended his action, saying that nothing concerning the indictment had been discussed. That of course was not the point. The point was that a President of the United States was presumably asking help or advice from a person whose former actions had been officially questioned.

As the newspeople left the conference I heard a man say to another that he did not think it was right for the President to have talked to Connally, then he added, "Connally could have written him anything he needed to know, but they shouldn't have been seen together."

That is admittedly an accepted scope of our morality, how things will look. People hear it all their lives, "How will it look if I go dressed like this?" or "How will it look if you are seen coming home at that hour?"

The newsman thought it would be acceptable for the President to receive information from Connally but not for them to talk together.
—February 18, 1975

*   *   *

The Bible, as you know, says that Eve, the first woman, was formed from a rib of Adam, the first man.

Now a Spanish biologist holds that woman is "a man whose development has been arrested, a sort of adolescent to whose organism is subjoined, in a kind of symbiosis, the apparatus of maternity, which is responsible for the check in development."

The Genesis account makes the point with fewer words.

—July 14, 1975

Love Songs

The themes of love songs have not changed, only the tempo, the times, the instruments and the singers. They tell of faithful, undying love, of lost love, of unrequited love, each generation in its own way.

There was the singer who vowed that for bonnie Annie Laurie, whose brow was like a snow-drift and whose throat was like a swan, the lass with the fairest face the sun ever shone down on, for her he would lay himself down and die.

"Believe Me if All Those Endearing Young Charms" is a delicate song in waltz time that declares undying love — let thy loveliness fade as it will, thou wouldst still be adored and so on. In passing it can be said it is doubtful that any aging lady, even still adored, would like to have her face described as "the dear ruins," but the sentiment is there and that is the main issue.

Or take that wistful "Long, Long Ago," the yearning of the singer to have things back the way they were — let me believe that you love as you loved, you told me you ne'er would forget.

Then there was the maiden whose heart was sore after Robin Adair's love had waned — now that thou'rt cold to me the town is dull, joy and mirth have fled and nothing is the same any more.

These romantic ballads were sung to the tinkling of a piano by young ladies in long dresses and young men in high collars in parlors by lamplight, a young man holding a lamp so the player and those clustered around the piano could see the words and music.

Now what you hear are songs belted out by bearded young men in tight pants and flowered shirts and beads and young ladies with stringing hair and exposed midriffs, accompanied by a twanging guitar, possibly amplified to thousands of decibels.

A girl wails that wishin' and hopin' won't get her into his arms or that she would rather live in his world than be without him in hers. A young man declares he never realized how happy she made him till he sent her away and now he's real sorry and wishes she was back. Another sings that his eyes adored her.

A singer asks wistfully if you would still need and still love him or her when age 64 is reached. That's an odd number to put in a song, not quite Social Security age and quite a ways from the "dear ruins" stage.

An uncertain young man sings that he has never loved before and wonders if he could make it without love, and a raucous voice screams for Bill Bailey to please come home.

And so it goes the world over, in any language, time without end — the sadness and gladness of Love.

—October 27, 1975

Chip a Bit Off

Dr. Tarlton Morrow, Jr. has some innovative thoughts about editing:

"Although I am not so naive as to think we could get along without editors, and whereas I am not making a blanket criticism of editors, why is it that the printed word can get changed but other art forms are not edited in the same way? I am thinking now of words that were written to have some artful impact. I suppose poems are not edited, but certainly prose is.

"The situation is analogous to a painter who would present a painting to be accepted by an art gallery and have a painting editor use some paint remover and take some spots out here and put some other color forms in there — and then call it editing the painting. The same thing might be said for a piece of sculpturing."

It's an amusing idea. Can't you imagine the indignation if an artist arrives at his or her own exhibition and finds the shadows in a painting have been lightened, the leaves darkened, roses made redder or paler? Or if a sculptor discovers that an art editor has chipped a bit off a nose or added a dimple to a chin?

Editors are clearly lords of all they survey, sitting at their desks and wiping out with their big blue pencils what may have been written in sweat and tears.

—December 6, 1975

Nannie Bingham

Kansas Day might bring a howling blizzard or it might bring balmy breezes, but in earlier years one thing it was sure to bring was Nannie Bingham. Nannie worked on the Sabetha Herald for some 50 years and in 1957 said she had not missed a Kansas Day dinner in Topeka in 53 years.

Why, dear readers, Nannie was coming to the banquets before the women were permitted to eat with the men, which was not until after 1922, when they got the vote. The ladies would eat a snack before they came, then climb the rickety stairs to the balcony of the old Masonic Building at 7th and Jackson.

There they sat and watched the men eat, smelled the food and listened to the speeches. Only one speaker ever so much as indicated they were in the building. When Homer Hoch as a young man gave the Ode to Kansas he looked up and referred to "the angels in the gallery."

When women got the vote they were not only permitted to eat with the men, but were allowed to hold office. It was understood that a woman would be elected vice president of the club, but the nomination was always made by a man and had to be seconded by a man from each district.

When Nannie held that office in 1932 she told the men that the reason the women pushed for suffrage was not so much that they wanted to vote, but that they wanted to eat.

—January 29, 1976

Summer Morning

The feel of a warm summer morning is filled with memories of other warm summer mornings in this place on Mulvane Street.

Walking with my husband to the sidewalk and watching him cut across the street on his way to work and coming to talk to my mother who had come out of the house with a hoe to chop a few weeds and loosen the dirt around her flowers.

"Plants have got to breathe," she said, hacking at the hard clayey ground and thinking perhaps of her loose sandy soil in the San Luis Valley and her wealth of flowers.

Sounds blended together, cars passing, a mail truck, a vacuum sweeper down the block. Women were getting at their work, sweeping walks, hanging out clothes, emptying the trash. The grass in the bright sunshine was yellow green, but under the trees a dark shadow. Even the cottonwood leaves barely moved in the still air.

From the alley came sounds of a hesitant motor. Our son and his friends were bending over his pride, his first car, a Model T chassis with the front seat still on. There was talk of valves and pistons while they listened as critically as a conductor to his musicians.

An ice truck stopped, dripping cool water as the iceman climbed the terrace steps bearing a large shining crystal cube to the house next door — a lovely sight and sound. But the iceman cometh no more.

From inside the house there was the tinkle of the piano as our daughter practiced her piano lesson from John Thompson's music book which her teacher marked with lop-sided stars for lessons well done.

She swung through Beethoven's Minuet, then on the Humoresque and another piece with a sad haunting melody that can still bring tears to my eyes. She put off playing Nola until last because she disliked it, with good reason, a prosaic, seesawy exercise.

The music came gently through the house out to where my mother and I were talking about what we would have for dinner.

"It's going to be a hot day," she would say.

Yes, it was going to be, but the morning was beautiful, filled with sights and sounds too exciting to leave for the company of a typewriter.

—June 2, 1976

Two Centuries

Looking about us we can ask what is the state of the nation brought forth two hundred years ago.

The continent has been settled, and inventions have brought a comfort and prosperity that could not have been imagined in 1776. Who then could have believed that news could be flashed instantly around the world and that a gavel in Rome, Italy could be heard in Rome, Georgia?

But what of the nation itself? Our present Congress comes off sadly in a comparison with the Second Continental Congress. Benjamin Rush, describing Samuel Adams, said, "His morals are irreproachable and even ambition and avarice, the usual vices of politicians, seem to have no place in his breast."

Ambition and avarice. Add to them complacency and expediency and you have what seems to be the current values.

Nothing like the Declaration of Independence had ever happened before. No colonies had ever before declared themselves free from their mother country.

In the hundred and fifty years on this new continent, far from the restrictions of the established royal system, the colonists had become a different people in a fresh land, a people come of age and impatient of the demands of an unjust parent. Feelings of freedom were in the air in the great land to the west.

It was a beginning — "We hold these truths to be self-evident." Where before in all the world had such truths been held to be self-evident, the truths that all men are created equal? All men, the Declaration said, not just the prominent and wealthy. Even the great Magna Carta spoke only for the barons. There was nothing in it about all men.

Where did those lofty and noble words of the Declaration come from except from new men on a new continent? They were words that were to give life and hope to other nations and bring new beginnings in far places.

—July 3, 1976

*   *   *

Zsa Zsa Gabor and I are a good deal alike. Zsa Zsa always has a husband and I always have a cat, but they may not be the same one from year to year.

—March 31, 1977

Bones of the Earth

I was on my way to Cottonwood Falls, drove west, crossed the Lyon County line, then more miles before seeing Strong City ahead, looking like a sweet Alpine village, the tall church spire rising among roofs and trees, and all set down in the surrounding hills.

The limestone Catholic church is a solid landmark that has served its people for many years. Then there was the Uptown theater, limestone, with twin steps leading to the front door.

As I proceeded toward Cottonwood Falls I seemed to be somewhere else. The road did not lead to the old bridge by the dam and into main street with the gem of the historic old courthouse at the end. Instead it crossed the Cottonwood River over a new bridge and came to the town a block east of the street. Men were fishing from the old bridge, as they always did on a Sunday or holiday. I was glad it was still there.

I drove to our old home near Bazaar, every curve of hill dear and familiar, a spaciousness of hill and sky that flowed into the mind and became a great canvas stretching from horizon to horizon and arching overhead.

The grass was lush and green, spreading out and turning to a blue haze in the distance. The South Fork of the river was outlined in the dark green of the trees, a color matched by cloud shadows on the grass.

Along the road could be seen the bones of the earth, the limestone layered by ancient seas. How did bluestem grass happen to grow in the thin soil that formed on those rocks?

The only sound that broke the solitude was the sweet pure song of the meadowlark. It was peace that quieted the need for praising it.

—July 9, 1977

Ingenuous

One evening when I was out for a little walk I came to a group of young children with a blond cocker spaniel. They asked if it was mine, said they had found it by a house but it didn't belong there.

We exchanged names, first names, and the children observed a ring I was wearing, the school class ring of the Center, Colo., high school, that had been my brother's.

They wanted to know if my brother lived with me. When I said he had died, an anguished look of grief came into the big brown eyes of a beautiful little girl who breathed, "Did your brother die!" Another said, "I wish nobody would ever die."

Other questions were asked. Did I have children? Why didn't they live with me? Did my grandchildren live with me? When, through elimination of children and grandchildren, they learned that nobody lived with me, they expressed sorrow and pity.

"Do you live all by yourself? We'll come and see you."

All of this conversation came just from seing for the first time six children on a street corner with a stray dog. Their questions were direct and interested.

Not one false word was spoken, not one insincere expression, not one word said just for politeness.

All too soon they will lose their sweet ingenuousness and learn the ways of civilized society.

—July 15, 1977

Elvis

He burst upon the world like a meteor shower, rained bright and dazzling sparks, and left as suddenly. The teenagers who screamed and moaned with delight are now married women who mourn silently.

Not only girls and women, but men, were worshipful admirers of Elvis Presley, and not only in this country, but all over the world. The country boy who strummed a guitar, self-taught, gyrated his hips and sang in a throaty provocative voice, reigned like a king and is as deeply mourned, more deeply, for there must be those who secretly rejoice when a king is gone.

Elvis Presley can not be explained. Conservatives dismissed him as brash and vulgar and unmusical, but when girls began screaming and people began buying his records by the millions, the Elvis Presley magic was established and he had only to appear, to touch a conflagration. His admirers wanted to see him, to hear him, to touch him, to have any object he touched, and many traveled all over the country to be at his concerts. They came by the thousands from far places to stand all night outside his home and mourn.

He was tender to an audience. Many have played better, sung better, danced better, but they lacked that indefinable mystery that brought it all together. It was much more than charm. Charm makes a person pleasing. Magic turns him into a dynamo. Elvis had magic, and he was kind, generous, humble, considerate, these despite a kind of sneering, mocking ironic air in his performance.

He must have been as astonished as the public when the girls began screaming — it is always the young who lead, the young who are free from inhibitions and open to the new. His admirers gave him, not a temporary acclaim, but devotion that was enduring for 20 years. This was extraordinary.

He made musical history and probably had more impact on the world than most kings.

Elvis had everything and died at the height of his power. Nobody knows what the future might have been, but his early death brought an end that was a blaze of glory.

If he had lived on and become old, his death might have evoked only memories instead of mourning.

May Williams Ward wrote a poem "My Little Sister," about a girl who had everything "blue eyes, pink cheeks, dimples and her hair curled."

She "played forward at basketball, shot ducks from cover, had a sweet rose-colored hat and a tall lover."

"All her life she had everything,
Plenty and more than plenty.
She did not need a perfect death.
Death at twenty."

None of us would call death at 20 a perfect death. Life is precious and we cling to it, even those who speak of mansions in the skies, but the poem has a mood and feeling.

—August 22, 1977

*   *   *

It occurs to me that a good many inventions come too late for their real need. Take radios, which made their appearance at a time when people already had good communication by telephone, newspapers and magazines and motor transportation.

But what a lot of help and comfort they would have brought to isolated pioneer families, if, along with the organ, sewing machine and grandma's marble-topped dresser, a radio could have been tucked into the covered wagon.

Then at night when the oxen were halted by dark, the radio would have brought news and music, drama and fun, keeping the weary travelers in touch with the world and possibly from growing a bit odd from loneliness.

Another thing that came too late is disposable diapers. Now, with automatic washers and driers, it would be nothing to run a load every day.

But back when water had to be carried from a spring, hauled from a creek or drawn from a well, they would have been handy. Women washed diapers on the washboard. Those pioneers could sure have used an automatic washing machine.

—October 3, 1977

Requiem

A requiem for Hubert Humphrey is Schiller's Hymn to Joy, set to music by Beethoven. It says that all men become brothers wherever the loving wings of joy are spread, that it embraces millions and is for the entire world, and above the starry sky dwells a loving father who makes all the men brothers. That is a very free translation given me by a friend whose native tongue is German.

Schiller lived during the French Revolution, which saw the end of the feudal system and brought the motto: Liberty, Equality, Fraternity. That could have been the theme of Hubert Humphrey's life.

He was happy and joyous, not as a person taking his pleasure remote from the world. Indeed, he was in the world and of the world, filled with dreams, hopes, plans, which he worked diligently to bring about. That he failed to reach his goal of becoming President is the nation's loss, but his life has touched hearts everywhere with his joy, his hope, his exuberance, a life full and running over that will reach farther than holding the high office.

181

Hubert Humphrey was a loving person. Casually we sign ourselves as loving, but not many really know how to love in a great joyous universal feeling for all mankind. He knew and it was in his voice, on his face, in his words, and he imparted some of it to the lives he touched.

Hubert Humphrey's life was a hymn to joy.

—January 19, 1978

*　　*　　*

Dr. Karl Menninger is a voice crying from the housetops for prison reform. He combines creative energy with a vision that sees far beyond the present and drives toward it. That drive was behind the reorganization of the State Hospital.

Shameful conditions exist in our prisons, he says, making them the opposite of their intended purpose, which is to rehabilitate. In a speech at the Kansas Sentencing Institute at Overland Park he asked fifty Kansas district court judges to spend 24 hours among the prisoners they have sentenced.

"It is very ugly and very sad and it will make you sick," he said.

Little by little the human race inches ahead, sometimes slipping back. The concept of individual freedom reached a peak in the new world when Thomas Jefferson declared that all men are equal.

The devices man has created for the punishment of his fellowman are unbelievably brutal and shockingly unjust. Dr. Menninger's book, "The Crime of Punishment," is a far-seeing look at a time when people, he said, "will take a less vindictive attitude toward law breakers."

—July 7, 1978

Logic

One thing that I learned about my great-granddaughter April is that she, and therefore any child her age, is logical. That this logic does not extend into adulthood is obviously the result of a child observing the illogical behavior of its elders.

Her grandfather brought her a little wooden doll bed he made. Immediately she tried to lie down on it. It was a bed. A bed is to lie on. Perfectly logical. When there was room only for her head she tried sitting on it. Fortunately I was there with my camera to record both actions.

Speaking of pictures, one day I took her sitting in a corner playing with her lamb. The next time she saw me with the camera she went and sat in the corner, which she concluded was a place for taking pictures.

One evening I was reading to her and rocking her to sleep and when I judged that desired stage had been reached, laid her temporarily on her parents' bed rather than risk waking her by bending down to the playpen, where she was sleeping since I crowded her out of her room. Dreamily she opened her eyes and pointed to the playpen, where she knew she belonged. I made the transfer and she went to sleep.

—July 15, 1978

Sir

Mr father-in-law, Elisha Barton Greene, was not born in Kansas, but no descendant of a pioneer who arrived in a covered wagon could have loved it more.

In Zanesville, Ohio, he was in the iron business. On our trip we were in that town and saw the big white house where he lived and where my husband was born. He was strong for the Presbyterian church, for prohibition and for farming, though he had never lived on a farm. The mecca that drew him to Kansas was the prohibition in this state. He didn't want his five sons and three daughters growing up where they sold whisky.

He loaded his household goods on a freight car and brought his family to Emporia, because the town had a Presbyterian college, then looked for a farm. When he was shown a farm in Chase County he took it, not because of the 500-acre pasture or the 400-acres of farm land, but because of the 13-room house, which would hold all his children.

Into this house some years later I came when I was married and had the fortunate experience of living in the house with him until his death, and my affection for him grew with the years. The house burned, the depression came, but he refused to go and live with his daughters, wanting only his own place in Kansas, whatever the hardships.

Rain might threaten with hay down or threshers might be in the field. No matter. There was always Bible reading and prayer before breakfast, with all the family and the hired man on their knees. No work or visiting was done on the Sabbath. A gray alpaca coat hung over his chair and he always put it on before sitting down to a meal, no matter how hot the day. He loved children and helped take care of ours. His sons addressed him as Sir and the neighbors as Mr.

—July 27, 1978

*   *   *

Beth Sheffel claims as her distinction that she shook hands four times with Einstein. When she was a child in Chicago he came to her school, and many were there to hear his talk and speak to him afterwards. Beth and some of her friends got in the line and worked their way up four times to shake hands.

Einstein looked at them, shook his head gently and said, "Kinder, kinder, genug."

—August 12, 1978

Second Morning

I stood on a little hill islanded in fog. I turned all around and looked and nothing but fog could be seen in any direction.

The hills and the valleys and the farms and the town were at the bottom of the filmy vapor that flowed out and touched the sky. Valleys and hills and farms are beautiful, but the soft gray haze billowing up like primordial mist was as fresh and cool and tranquil as sleep.

Strange that it is said of a bewildered and confused man that he is in a fog. In a fog it is quiet and calm, nothing to bewilder or confuse. Ugliness and harshness and glare are clouded in a soft gray filter and you are alone in your little island.

Out of the still came the clear rapture of a bird. Unseen, a crow cawed.

This must have been the way the world looked on the morning of the second day, when the light had been divided from the darkness, and the firmament set in the sky. All around there was mist and formless void, with one little place cleared for the Creator to stand and work.

Here was stuff to make an earth. Easy now — it must be a good one, a beautiful, long-enduring, everlasting, imperishable one. I think it was surely a breath-taking sight, the mist and darkness waiting to be made into a world.

Perhaps it was begun a little reluctantly, and late in the second day, but it was carved and divided, scooped out and pushed up, smoothed and leveled and drained, then colonized.

Long, long, long ages afterwards, when the Lord sees the scars and gashes on the earth, and that the man and the woman never learned wisdom after all, He must sometimes remember back to that joyous second morning, cool and rapturous in the mists, clean and new and untouched.

And He must sometimes wonder if He may not have made a mistake.

—October 5, 1978

*　　*　　*

So the president has fired Bella Abzug. The surprise is that he appointed her. Bella is an energetic woman who has her place in the world. She is one who has to be out front, being heard, plowing new ground, giving the word. She is not the kind to fit into an administration in which others are expected to do the talking.

—January 31, 1979

Nuclear Accident

"Nobody was hurt, nobody has been killed." These were the words of an official of the Metropolitan Edison Co. in an effort to minimize the accident at the Three Mile Island nuclear plant in Pennsylvania, which is owned by the company.

That defense has been used many times, that nobody has ever been killed at a nuclear plant. The number of lives lost have in the past marked the extent of a disaster. But man has brought a new danger upon himself, a danger that can not be seen or heard or felt or smelled. It is the danger of excessive radiation.

A disaster may occur at a coal mine. An oil well may catch on fire. Chemicals may explode at a manufacturing plant. Factories may burn. people may be killed or injured. Damage to property may be high.

184

But such accidents do not make the air dangerous to breathe up to a possible 20 miles distance. They do not cause anxiety over possible birth defects, cancer and sterility in the years ahead. They may be tragic disasters, but the results can be seen and known and dealt with.

Anything that is built can cause trouble. It can come from defective material, from careless workmanship, improper inspection, or it can just come for no reason. And any person can make mistakes. Despite training, supervision and precautions, human error occurs, and one error by one person can turn into a tragedy.

The accident at Three Mile Island is reported to have resulted from both mechanical failure and human error. An early news story told of similar trouble that had occured at the plant some months ago, about which the operators had been warned.

One official said, "When we started with nuclear energy, we knew there would be risks."

Every venture involves risks—a risk of money, often the money of many people, a risk of future debts. To risk money is one thing, but risking danger to the air we breathe, to water, to the very earth itself is another. This is the reason for the grave concern felt by many people about nuclear plants. Even if no accidents occur, nuclear plants still involve danger.

Much of the concern is for the unsolved problem of nuclear waste disposal. It is not ordinary waste, but radioactive material that can be a danger for thousands of years in the future. A recent report told of deep-sea divers finding casks breaking, casks in which early waste had been stored and dumped in the ocean. No device or material can resist erosion in land or sea for the life of nuclear waste. It could seep into undergroud streams, be dislodged by earthquakes.

Tons of waste are now stored waiting government plans for disposal. If nuclear plants increase, it means that every year new tons of waste will accumulate and wait for disposal. Getting it out of sight is not getting it out of potential danger.

A person has a right to risk his money, even his health and life. But we should ask ourselves if anyone has the right to risk danger to future generations, to risk contamination of earth and air and water for a million years in the future.

—April 5, 1979

Infare

Last week I had occasion to recall the word "infare." A niece in California, Mary Virginia Murphy, sent us a couple of pieces of beautiful fine old china, a sugar bowl and a plate, decorated with pink flowers and a gold design.

They are from the "infare china" bought by grandparents of my husband for the infare dinner of his parents. Elisha Barton Greene and his

185

bride, Virginia Moore. The grandparents who held the infare dinner and bought the china were William Moores of Portsmouth, Ohio.

William's parents met as romantically as Jacob and Rachel, according to family annals: "Young, good-looking Levi Moore, a son of Philip of the stone house, came by on horseback and, stopping at the home of Samuel Gunn, asked for a drink of water. It was brought to him by Samuel's daughter, Amanda. It seems to have been a case of love at first sight, for not long afterwards they were married."

Amanda bore 10 children, three of whom died in infancy. At age 22 when William, her oldest, was born, in 1815, she put on a cap and wore one for the rest of her life. She died in 1888 at 95, the age at which both her mother and her grandmother had died.

When she was old, her grandchildren loved to go to her room and listen to stories of early days. She told of the little sister who fell from the wagon as they were crossing the mountains and had to be left in a tiny roadside grave; of pioneer life in a log cabin when matches were unknown and families kept a perpetual fire and if the fire went out, a child with as iron kettle was sent to a neighbor's for live coals; of the spinning and weaving of cloth for clothes and blankets; of moving from the log cabin into the nice new house they built on the beautiful Ohio River. Her mother had brought out from Connecticut a long, scarlet felt circular coat with an ermine collar, a coat which the grandchildren used many times for plays and charades.

When I was first married and came to the home of my husband's parents near Bazaar, my new in-laws acquainted me with family history. I remember the pieces of the infare china and also of china from the Steamer Hope, the name of the river boat owned by William Moore. He and his brothers owned boats they ran down the Ohio and the Mississippi to New Orleans, boats that carried both passengers and freight.

The poet, Marianne Moore, was the wife of one of William's sons, Milton, for whom my husband was named. He was Miltron Willard Greene. His mother added the Willard because she admired Frances Willard.

"Infare" is a word not heard much anymore. The dictionary defines it as "A feast and reception for a newly married couple usually at the home of the groom's family a day or two after the wedding."

I remember that word as a child. Infares were popular in our part of the state, a farming community of small towns. Few couples took wedding trips. It was customary for the bride and groom to spend their first night at the home of the bride's parents, and go to the groom's parents the next day for the infare. A bride had a wedding dress and an infare dress. That was in my mother's generation.

—May 30, 1979

Planet Earth

The greatest mystery on this planet is the planet itself. Wouldn't you think that it would be so fascinating that people would talk about it wherever two or three were gathered together?

Instead of going on about the price of gasoline, hogs or coffee; instead of reporting when the girl next door came home the night before; instead of telling how the beauty operator ruined your hair with that inferior dye; instead of speculating on who will win the pennant; it would seem that people would be exchanging views on how the earth got started, where people and animals and trees came from and where and when and why and how it would all end.

Scientists speak grandly of big bangs, of an exploding universe, of space and void, but nobody can go back to the beginning, to what caused the big bang, what set off the exploding universe, where space ends, where void begins.

Something does not start from nothing. Genesis says that in the beginning God created the heaven and the earth, but not a word about the material used. All this great variety was made from a stated number of chemical elements plus the breath of life.

This planet and the life on it are the great mysteries that no Sherlock Holmes or Miss Marple or Nero Wolfe could unravel. If I don't find the answer in another existence I am going to be awfully disappointed.

Every group of people has invented myths about The Beginning. A Chinese legend has the creator of the universe a being called P'am Ku. Assisted by a dragon, a unicorn, a phoenix and a tortoise, he labored 18,000 years chiseling the earth into its present shape. (Not six days, but 18,000 years.)

When he died his flesh became the world's soil, his blood its rivers, his sweat the rain, his hair the trees and plants. His left eye turned into the sun, his right eye into the moon, his breath became the wind and his voice the thunder. And the parasites on his body became members of the human race — a sly, wry commentary.

A nobler conception was man made in the image of the creator. One concept makes nature the important creation, another gives the honor to man.

But all people everywhere have felt the majesty of a Beginning, of a Creator, of the power and the glory and have made their legends and stories. They have felt themselves a part of the great mystery, have visioned the union of gods and mortals.

My grandson David asked questions about beginnings and when I kept saying I did not know, he fell silent and I feared he was thinking that I had learned very little in my many years of living.

But all he said was, "When I grow up, I am going to find out." I have not checked with him lately, but I expect to see him this summer.

—June 23, 1979

We Care Very Much

On the front of a catalog I received was a letter, very personal and friendly. It said "What ever happened to our friends, the Greenes?

"Mrs. Greene, is everything all right? We have never heard from you. Although we have been sending you catalogs faithfully.

"If we don't hear from you very soon we will have to say good-bye forever to the Greenes and that would be a crying shame, because WE CARE VERY MUCH ABOUT YOU, MRS. GREENE."

I was touched by such concern for our family and am sending them this letter:

"Dear Mrs. Spencer — It sure was awful nice of you to write me a special letter right along with your catalog. Nothing much has happened. We are all tolerable well and hope it finds you the same. I'm sorry you are worried, but then I'm not much of a hand at letter writing, or sending away for things.

"Money is getting kind of tight here, just melts away. A little sack of groceries costs you $10, then there's the gasoline and all those miscellanies. This summer there was the last half of the taxes on our house and in July the insurance was due on both the house and the car. Course it wasn't much on the car, which is 12 years old and still running good, but the house insurance has gone way up. You wouldn't believe it and the house a year older at that.

"Not long ago I had to have a new roof and this year I had to have the garage painted. A few weeks ago I had to have the electrician and the man to keep my oven from running away with itself. Right this minute there is a drippy faucet in the bathroom and I ought to have the plumber fix it.

"I have looked through your catalog to see what we might send off for. I guess we could use the toenail clipper, but don't need any corn or bunion attachment. I don't have my ears pierced, so can't use your playing card earrings. I have already got some beads, so I don't need your 'Try Jesus' necklace, nor your twin make-up mirror. Do you know I can comb my hair without even looking into a mirror, before or after?

"Your bath-tub pillow and mat might be nice, but would be trouble to dry out. I just rest my head against a towel when I want to stretch out. The porcelain swan is real pretty, but I already have a knicknack or two. I have plenty of spoons and don't need your flower-of-the-month set, nor any china cats. I've got a live one. I don't need your 'Nobody's Perfect' T-shirt to call attention to my lacks, nor your comic bathroom tissue. We just use a plain color, without jokes.

"Maybe along toward Christmas I might send in an order for a few things. Now you all take care of yourselves."

—August 31, 1979

188

La Grippe

I have been laid low with influenza or as we used to say, La Grippe. I wouldn't say I have wrestled with it but rather that I have endured it for a week. My father treated it with quinine, my mother with hot lard and turpentine spread on the chest and covered with a hot flannel cloth. I have two kinds of medicine from my doctor to take one of each three times a day.

Influenza is not excruciatingly painful. A dull ache takes over the body, an ache through which events and duties are seen through a veil darkly. La Grippe blunts interest in outside matters and responsibility toward work.

At first it was not unpleasant to lie back in the big chair covered with an afghan and read, with no nagging sensation that I should be up and about some useful work.

I went through a murder mystery, not a good one. It was about a beautiful young blonde girl spaced out on drugs because her parents did not understand her. They wanted her to go to a good school and enjoy opportunities. It wasn't her thing — it was not made clear just what her thing was — so the solution was for her to run away from home and get on drugs. That seems to be the way the young people are handling their problems these days.

About the second or third day I got tired of reading. Nothing invited my interest. I did not want poetry or politics. I ran my eyes over rows of books, declined Maeterlinck's Life of the Bee and of the White Ant. I rejected Freud, had no interest in the Right People or Man of the Future. I was concerned with my aches and pains and couldn't be bothered by outside ideas.

I just lay with my eyes closed and tried to keep from swallowing. It was painful to swallow, yet something impelled me to swallow. I sipped juice to take the dry bitter taste out of my mouth.

I brought in the papers but did not turn beyond the front pages. I turned on the television and through a veil heard about the hostages and the elections. Lawrence Welk came on and when he was followed by Billy Graham, I just let it run on, too listless to turn it off.

Maybe it could not be said I was enjoying my misery, but I was certainly wallowing in it, lying in bed most of the afternoon and soaking in hot baths. I lost contact with time. What seemed to be evening would turn out to be three o'clock.

Then it occurred to me that perhaps I ought to eat something. It is hard to have a satisfactory illness when one is alone in a house, with nobody to smooth pillows, fold blankets, cluck in sympathy and bring food.

Yet I was not without comfort. Goodie, my cat, was with me. She came and sat by me in the big chair and when I lay on the davenport she was beside me, to be patted and rubbed.

Today on the sixth day I woke with a sense of duty. I remembered I had left clothes in the dryer, that I had work to do. Though still weak and achy, the veil is gone and I am face to face with duty. It must be the final stages of La Grippe.

—March 14, 1980

*   *   *

Dear Shareholder," said the letter from a corporation, "During the first fiscal quarter of 1980, which ended Jan. 31, your fund continued to show that its portfolio, as structured and managed, is extremely responsive to positive forces in its area of investment concentration."

Is that good news or bad?

—March 15, 1980

*   *   *

My neighbor, 10-year-old Andrew McHenry, has become an authority on baseball, and in only about a year's time. He can tell you who plays where on what team, his batting average and anything else you might want to know.

He managed to insult both his mother, Susan, and me in one sentence. Susan asked, in all innocence, "What does it mean when they say they fanned a player?" With a mixture of scorn and pity, Andrew said, "Even Peggy knows that."

—October 23, 1980

Baseball

Ken LaZebnik is equally at home writing plays or sports articles. Besides his involvement in the Mixed Blood Theatre in Minneapolis, he publishes a little quarterly magazine, the Minneapolis Baseball Review. In his first issue, winter 1981, called the Hot Stove edition, starting the season at home, he wrote about his strong opposition to splitting the leagues into three divisions.

"One of the glories of the baseball fan," he said, "is following his team through the majestic span of a season. Like explorers of a new world, we discover with our team, hills and valleys, streaks and slumps that we could not have guessed at in the spring. What's this? A gorge of defeat so soon on the trek. Don't worry. It's a long season. A good team will rise to the top.

"Baseball is a game which unfolds majestically over 162 games to determine excellence. It is a heart-breaking game because it has no mercy — there is only one winner. Rightfully so. It grabs our hearts and minds because of its relentless pursuit of excellence: a pennant race is thrilling because only one team will occupy first place."

—March 27, 1981

*   *   *

I turned on the television and there was that gorgeous young beauty popping a drop of that magical "oil of delay" (it delays old age) on her exquisite skin."

—April 14, 1981

Easter Finery

Sunday is the day toward which choirs and seamstresses, florists and hairdressers, grocers and egg dyers have been aiming in a crescendo of pleasant activity.

Churches will be filled with people wearing new clothes. Some of them may not have been inside a church since last Easter. Yet they will come, without embarrassment or apology, just as radiant and happy as the others.

Regular church attendants will be in their places as usual, in new apparel or old. It makes no difference. They may feel slightly complacent as the visitors fill the church, perhaps even a bit scornful — oh, not sinful scorn, just a kind of amused, intellectual scorn. They may be thinking that the unaccustomed worshipers have come only to show off their new clothes.

But they will be wrong.

Wearing a new spring outfit to church on Easter morning is a tradition, and traditions are backed up by strong feelings and good reasons.

New clothing is worn on important occasions. It is not vanity that causes a bride to choose a beautiful gown for her wedding, nor that makes the mother of the bride want to have a new and becoming dress. Women presented to the Queen of England are expected to appear in fine raiment with three ostrich feathers in their hair. A girl wants a new dress for that special prom at college and the wife of a new president chooses something very nice for his inauguration.

New or special clothes are a way of honoring an occasion, a way of recognizing and expressing its importance.

Easter is a joyous day, made more so by its movable date, depending on the moon and the vernal equinox. The earth is renewing itself. Grass has returned and every flower, shrub and tree has put on its finest.

It is a time for people to renew their lives and each person needs many resurrections. People get shut away in the darkness of discouragement, pain, hopelessness, defeat, apathy, fear and forget how bright it could be if they would come into the sunshine.

Resurrection is for those who have the faith to see hope bursting out of the darkness and for those who have the courage to believe and accept the miracle of change.

Resurrection is the belief in a new life, to leave behind the darkness of sorrow, roll away the stone and walk out into the sunlight.

—April 18, 1981

*   *   *

You can't win an argument with an editor, as John Ripley can testify. The editor has the copy and the big red pencil.

In an article he wrote for American Heritage, he used the word "plush," to denote elegance. In the galley proof sent him the word had been changed to "posh." He marked out "posh" and wrote in his own word, "plush," and sent the copy back.

That went on for two or three more exchanges, the young lady editor insisting on her word, which was the one used in the final article.

—April 21, 1981

Blessed Little Rebels

It is young children who have courage. They stand up to giants who have absolute physical power over them and vent their angers in passionate outbursts. They do not soften the words with flattery, make concessions or appeasements.

They speak plainly and defiantly to these hulking powerful monsters. They accuse them in plain simple words. They defend themselves, protect injustices. They leave no possibility to doubt their feelings.

Blessed little rebels.

Too soon they will grow up and learn to be discreet and expedient. They will understand the advantages of being diplomatic, will calculate the outcome. They will take notice of which side of their bread is spread with the popular substitute.

Glorious little rebels, facing up to these behemoths in teary protest, little Davids with slingshot words. Their feelings of injustice expressed in torrents of frustrated anger.

A child has the courage to put up a fight when his expectations are disrupted, the courage and will to defy someone who has power over him. No beating about the bush, no fear of consequences, no talking behind the giant's back. The stream of words flows freely, face to face, with the ring of a righteous cause.

Truth is spoken as it is seen — each person sees his own truth — truth without rancor, without fear, one person to another, temporarily as equals. And afterwards no hint of bitterness or resentment, nothing that needs to be explained or forgiven.

The little rebels accept conciliation from the powerful ones, permit the wiping of tears, the bestowing of kisses, the rocking, held gently in the arms of their recent adversary. It is a peace accepted as naturally as their tears of protest.

Honest little rebels.

When they reach that longed-for state of adulthood, they will understand that it is often the better part of wisdom to leave some feelings unexpressed. They may find it desirable to swallow their thoughts in the presence of some physically inferior creature who holds economic or political power. They will learn to remain silent when it seems expedient to do so.

Their crystal stream of words will not flow so freely and will be tempered with consideration. Or if it does flow freely and passionately, nothing held back, and does not fit current popular opinions, these grown-ups may be labeled radicals, extremists, reactionaries, fanatics.

But for a few magnificent years they are glorious, honest, fearless, righteous little rebels.

—May 8, 1981

*   *   *

After Matt, their second child was born, my granddaughter Joyce said that her husband, Dennis, going to the store, would ask, "What do you want besides milk and diapers?"

—May 28, 1981

A Good Friend Lost

Goodie is dead, and I am filled with pain and grief. She was born in this house, and we lived here together for more than 13 years. She was a member of the family, loved by all of us. I miss her every day.

Mornings after she ate she would come and lie on the newspaper, right where I was reading. When I turned a page she would move, then settle back again.

I miss her eager face outside the door, mornings after she had been outside all night, her face uplifted expectantly. If she was not there and did not come soon, I was out looking for her and calling her name. Then suddenly, from I knew not where, she would be there beside me.

Before she was a year old she began climbing a tree in the yard, up to high branches and from there to a neighbor's roof, a high roof, two stories and an attic. Men climbed ladders to get her down, then when they reached for her, she cooly drew back. On a cold New Year's Eve she was up there all night, crying for help. In the morning I had her rescued.

She stopped going to that roof and climbed another tree to the roof of our sun porch, from where I could rescue her through a bedroom window. She announced her need with loud meowing, and gave a low meow as she was lifted inside.

She was soft and furry, gray with black markings, long tail held aloft. Her face was beautiful, brownish eyes, delicate gray nose, long white whiskers.

She was never too old to play, would jump at any moving object, including scissors I was using. Our neighbor Andrew called her, "The fastest paw in the West." Even when she was sick she would reach a beautiful soft paw for a length of red yarn.

Mornings I would often wake to find her on my bed and she flowed down the stairs ahead of me, wanting her breakfast. She would walk away from canned food. She liked liver and kidney, fish and hamburger, milk and cream and cottage cheese.

When she became sick she would eat nothing. I fed her with a spoon and held her on my lap, wrapped in a soft shawl. She lay quietly, making no sound and when I smoothed her fur and called her name, she gently moved her tail in response.

Goodie had no houses or land, no stocks or jewels. She had only herself and needed nothing more. She was an ornament to the house and a joy to its occupants. Many others loved her. She lived in pleasure, in confidence, in dignity, a shining mark.

We buried her by the rambler rose I brought from my old home in Missouri. Goodie was dear to me and I am full of grief and pain.

—November 5, 1981

Turkeys

On the Missouri farm where I grew up my mother raised turkeys. They shared the barnlot with the chickens, but did not share their way of living. The turkey had not made friends with the people, had not surrendered his own ways as the chickens had. He was still more wild than tame.

The turkey hen disdained the rows of prepared nests into which a chicken hen stepped when she felt an egg-laying coming on. The turkey hen stole quietly away to make a nest in a secret, secluded place, to keep her eggs and eventually her young from the enemy.

My mother had plans for the eggs, to gather them, hatch them and raise the young. The money they brought in the fall helped pay the taxes and buy winter clothes for the family. One year they bought a wonderful, six-octave organ, but that is another story.

So she assigned my brother and me to trail the turkey hen and find where she had hidden her nest. We were instructed to make no noise and stay far behind her. Across the road from our house was a woods, the perfect place to hide a nest.

A reason given for the turkey's ingenious hiding of her nest is that the gobbler of the species has not learned the rudiments of fatherhood and is disposed toward breaking the eggs. Why would he want to break the eggs? To eat? Or for a darker motive?

No private eye tailing a suspect could have been more excited on discovering his rendezvous than we were when we saw the turkey stop, raise her head to look around for any lurking enemy, then settle down on her nest. We ran back to report, and though we should have felt like spies and traitors, we thought of ourselves as the bringers of good news. We were on our mother's side, not the turkey's.

The eggs were quietly removed from the nest, with a spoon—it was thought that the turkey would know the touch of hands — and kept until there were enough for a setting. The innocent turkey had not learned to count. The ultimate insult was when her eggs were put beneath a chicken hen to be hatched, as they sometimes were. The young turkey is very delicate, subject to roup, and whole hatchings sometimes died. The turkey hen had her troubles, which also became the troubles of her owner.

194

We loved the dear little striped creatures that came out of the large speckled eggs, and grew so fast we could almost see them leaving off down and putting on feathers. We were delighted at the first gobbles of the adolescent toms.

In the fall when they were sold a few were held back, in addition to the breeding stock. One was marked for Thanksgiving. I felt a distant tinge of sorrow when I saw him strutting proudly about the yard, practicing his gobble, blissfully unaware of his fate.

I felt a kind of sadness, but not sad enough to abstain from the feast. I was not a worthy advocate. I was still on my mother's side, and on my own, the flesh stronger that the spirit.

—November 26, 1981

Memories to Cherish

Oscar Stauffer lived a real life story that outdid the old tales of poor boy makes good. He came into this century at age 14 and was soon making his way in the world. It let to his ownership of 20 daily newspapers, two television stations, nine radio stations and other affiliated operations in 11 states, an empire of publishing.

It may have been chance that he became interested in newspapers. He came to Emporia from Hope — where he was born Nov. 26, 1886 — to finish high school. His mother had died when he was four, his father when he was 12, and a loving stepmother had taken over the family.

At Emporia he worked for William Allen White on the Gazette, a fortunate turn for the young man, for White urged him to go to college for more education. During his two years at the University of Kansas, he was again in touch with a newspaper, the Kansas City Star.

But his success was within himself, in his strong will and spirit, and I do not dcubt that in whatever he may have chosen to do, he would have been equally successful. His will and spirit were embellished with other qualities that led to his success, a generous dealing with people, his policy that his papers continue serving their communities just as they had before his ownership, and his feeling that people must change with the times.

At his first paper, the Peabody Gazette-Herald, he found that a good many were receiving the paper without having paid for it. He wrote them, stating the facts and saying they may not have subscribed for the paper in the first place and allowing them to be judge and jury. If they wished, he would forget the past and start them new.

That was a diplomatic and generous offer. The people came in and 96 percent ended up paying for all arrears.

In Peabody he stood for hours and fed type into the press by hand. His big press at The Capital-Journal almost runs itself and not a Linotype is used any more. He changed with the times. Something new was always being installed at the paper.

He came into the century at a time of change. People were beginning to use automobiles, electricity was being put to new uses, and there was talk of flying machines. Then came that wonderful device that brought voices out of the air and later a still more magical one that brought not only the voices, but the people's images into one's home.

Mr. Stauffer was busy these years, not only with his publishing, but with work for many state and community organizations. For many years he served on the Board of Regents. He was a trustee of the Menninger Foundation, Washburn University, Midwest Research Foundation, Agricultural Hall of Fame, his church and others.

He took time off to launch Alf Landon as a candidate for president in 1936 and Landon thinks if he had continued to work in the campaign, indeed had been made head of it, that he would have done better that two states.

Mr. Stauffer gave large sums of money to KU, Washburn, hospitals and schools. He traveled and did important work on journalism committees.

Mr. Stauffer denied being a self-made man, insisting that many people helped him, just as he in his life has helped many people.

—March 1, 1982

Well Dressed Chicken

This is a story about the chicken that went to market in a shirt. It was told to me by Bea Johns, who lived across the street when we first moved to this house.

As a child she lived on a farm with her parents, Edward and Chettie Kassebaum. One day a chicken that had no feathers was hatched. It shivered in the cold and was chilled in the rain. The other chickens, seeing that it was different from themselves, pecked it until it was raw and bleeding.

Chettie took pity on the poor thing, carrying on bravely and avoiding the other chickens as much as it could. Then it came to her what she could do for it. She could make it a shirt.

She cut tubular sections from the arms and legs of her husband's wornout underwear, knitted material that could, when cuts were made for the wings, slip on easily over the body. The unfortunate chicken had suffered not only from its peers, but had been burned by the hot sun.

"The chicken didn't know what to do about its shirt," Bea said. "It looked back to get a better view of it and tried to reach it with its bill to pull it off. But my mother took a few stitches in any shirt that seemed loose. She cut a clean shirt and changed it every day."

When the chicken got used to the shirt, it seemed to enjoy it and made no struggle when a clean one was put on.

But a strange thing happened when the other chickens noticed the shirt. Before, the chicken had been different, but not too different to belong and to be punished for its difference.

Now it was different in another way, scary different, strange enough to make the others afraid of it, as though in some manner it had been given

196

an unnatural change. They stopped pecking it and began another kind of punishment. They avoided it. Creatures of all kinds are afraid of the supernatural.

The chicken was growing, but still no feathers came. So when it was time to be sold, it went off to market with the others, in a clean shirt.

—May 8, 1982

My Father

My father, Jacob Anders Bennington, was a school teacher in his earlier years and a great believer in education, particularly in mathematics. He encouraged us to excel, my sister Julia and me as well as our brother George, the youngest. There are fathers who are firm and strict with their sons, but think of a daughter as a treasure to be pampered and indulged.

Not our father. He was ahead of his time in women's rights. He consulted my mother in whatever he did. We grew up thinking of men and women as equals, but different, each contributing in his or her own way.

My father was a member of the school board of our Union country school and was often the member who came on the last Friday afternoon of the month to bring the teacher her pay check. I wish now I had known how much it was. Wages and salaries had scant interest for a child in a community where everybody farmed and their money came from the produce they sold. I doubt that the teacher got more than $25 a month.

When my father came to school I was both shy and proud. The other children would look at me and grin. A parent was rarely in the schoolroom.

On Fridays the teacher often allowed the pupils to cipher or "spell down" after the last recess instead of having classes. Two pupils chose up sides and competed against each other.

On one of my father's visits we were having a ciphering match. At the blackboard the children would add by the dot system, translating each digit into dots, making an exciting sound of chalk on the blackboard.

When the teacher asked her usual question of visitors, if they wanted to say anything, my father arose and asked if he might show them another way to add, and proceeded with a simple talk about the combination of numbers.

My father was a restless man. An air of melancholy hovered about him, sometimes a quiet wistfulness, sometimes a remote detachment. He was lean and in summer so tanned that his intensely blue eyes looked like turquoises in a terra cotta setting. His straw hat left a line across his forehead that marked the end of the tan. His high cheek bones were emphasized by the hollows beneath them.

He was a worrier. "Now Mag, look after the children and don't let them . . ." was a familiar line. He feared that Julia and I might catch our dresses on fire if we washed dishes with the pan on the stove. He feared we might fall into the well if we drew up water. He would leave the house with his usual warning, then sometimes return with another. Or even the same one.

My mother was patient and understanding and loving. I never heard harsh words pass between them. I never doubted that they would always be there and would provide for anything I might need.

He called me Hon and liked for me to comb his hair while he read. He was interested in anything that happened anywhere. In a paper he came across the picture of a woman in a dress almost backless and showed it to my mother, while making mild noises of disapproval at such scandalous exposure, then added, "She does have a nice plump back."

—June 19, 1982

Attitude

ERA supporters, should dry their tears and take a look at history. Also, have a look at the nation's attitude toward the Constitution, which is patriotically evoked any time a phrase, in or out of context, seems to uphold something that is desired, but that is questionable.

The Constitution itself is something like the mother who tells her child several times to stop what he is doing, but he goes right ahead until finally she repeats her order, adding, "And I mean it this time."

In 1865 an amendment to the Constitution, Article XIII, freed the slaves. In 1868 another amendment, Article XIV, said that "all persons born or naturalized in the United States are citizens of the United States and of the state wherein they reside." Furthermore, it said, "No state shall make or enforce any laws which shall abridge the privileges or immunities of citizens of the United States."

That should have done it, the slaves freed and made citizens. But the Constitution repeated itself. In 1870 Article XV said the right of any citizen to vote should not be denied because of "race, color or previous condition of servitude."

Yet within the last few weeks the Voting Rights Act has again come up and again been signed by the president and renewed — 114 years after the Constitution had seemingly made the issue ironclad.

So I greatly doubt that those few words ERA supporters longed to see in the Constitution about no right being denied on account of sex would make much difference in the lives of women. We have already gained a great deal and I have an idea that anything we get in the future will be through our own efforts.

The black people and their friends and supporters had to struggle for the simple fundamental right of going to polls and casting vote. And now, more than a century later, it is thought that special laws are still needed to ensure their right to vote.

Putting words into the Constitution does not seem to make a great difference. Whatever a majority of the people want, they will get, no matter what the Constitution says, and they will have help from the judges and lawyers. The prohibition law is another example of the people doing what they want to do, regardless of the Constitution.

—July 8, 1982

Adventure

Last Sunday Mabel Remmers and I drove to the lake looking for a shady place for a picnic and saw empty tables at the Yacht Club. Neither of us belongs to the Yacht Club, but the people were friendly and made us welcome.

Young families with children were there, with boats coming and going, their tall white sails beautiful in the water. We were near the cliff promontory with the Gazebo at the point, where Mabel used to come with a book and sit and read.

We were having a delightful time, talking to the nice young sailing people. Then one of the men asked, "Would you like to go sailing?" Would we! We had not imagined the little expedition to the lake to eat a sandwich would mean an invitation to sail.

He was Fred Starrett, who with his wife, Linda, races their boat, which has two sails and is called a scow. He said that in last week's race they lost a little time when he fell out of the boat.

Mabel and I put on life jackets and got into the boat with Fred. She was given the mainsail rope and I the jib, to be tightened or loosened at the captain's order — a sailing lesson as well as a ride. We sailed out into the lake, "coming around," and doing other maneuvers and enjoying the sights and sounds and feels of wind and water.

It just shows that you never know what adventure is ahead. All you need do is meet it halfway.

—July 24, 1982

Equal

Harry Truman left an article, written in 1958, expressing fear that the world would be destroyed by nuclear fire.

He urged the leader of some strong nation to go to the General Assembly of the United Nations and advocate international control of nuclear energy. This person, he said, should advocate an international police force to control the bomb and maintain peace all over the world, which he said was faced with total destruction "unless the great leaders of the world prevent it."

Yet he, as a great leader of the world, was the first, and only, person to order the use of atomoic weapons in war. Now, at the 37th anniversary of its use at Hiroshima, we read of the devastations still being caused by radiation from that bomb, which killed, disfigured and may be sending its destruction to children yet unborn.

Truman justified the use of the bomb — it would bring the war to an end, would save the lives of many military people engaged in fighting the war.

Whoever might use the bomb in any future war, bombs many times more destructive than the Hiroshima bomb, would undoubtedly find some reason to rationalize its use — one might be about to lose a war and think that only the use of the bomb would turn the tide. Like Truman, they too would find some excuse.

But now many nations have the bomb, and would retaliate with bombs, bringing death and destruction.

Why else are they making the bombs? Why are we all spending billions of dollars on something so deadly and destructive? On something that creates waste that nobody wants and that can remain dangerous for a thousand years?

Now, only 37 years later Truman's own country and its former ally are engaged in a deadly race of atomic bombs — if not for use, then what for? They say they must keep even with each other, that only the fear of retaliation will prevent their use. Surely it must be the greatest madness that has been seen in all time.

There is a way to be equal and to save the billions of dollars now being spent, money that could be used for health and education, homes, roads, research on disease.

Zero bombs would be equal — to zero bombs.

—August 23, 1982

Great Occasion

It was a night to remember — two great men coming together at Washburn University for the first Karl Menninger Lecture — Dr. Karl and Norman Cousins, the first lecturer.

They are not men who have put together a great conglomerate of industries or manipulated the stock market, but men who have turned their talents toward the service of mankind. Both are concerned with the total good, believing that mental health and physical health go together as a whole. Both are concerned about the people saving themselves from the folly and tragedy of the bomb build-up.

They are certain that both the Russian people and the people in this country want peace and want the fruits of their labor to be used for education and a better living, not for destruction. There was talk of working for a United Nations with authority to keep peace.

Almost every seat in the hall was filled. The people knew this was a great occasion.

—October 7, 1982

Struggle for Rights

For his Ph.D at Harvard, Thomas C. Cox, who lived in Topeka in earlier years, chose the subjects of "Blacks in Topeka, Kansas, 1865-1915." It was published by the Louisiana State University Press. The book shows diligent research of newspapers in Topeka, particularly black newspapers, census reports, political documents and personal papers.

After the blacks had been freed from slavery and after amendments to the Constitution had made them citizens specifically mentioning that they should be denied no rights because of race, color or previous condition of servitude, they must have reasonably expected to take their place among other citizens.

Here they were with the freedom they had dreamed of and longed for. But they found closed doors and high walls and were to struggle many a painful year to obtain the simple right to mingle equally with the other citizens of this country. More than ever they must have expected that in Kansas, which fought for their freedom, they would be welcomed as citizens.

But let it be said for them that struggle they did. This book is a documented study of their will and spirit, their determination and perserverance in their efforts to secure their rights.

Let it be said, too that there were many here in high places who rejected discrimination. One of the first was John Burris, who said, "We must proceed on the assumption that blacks are to live in common with whites. Accordingly, they should be made as intelligent and as moral as education can make them." William Hutchinson at the Wyandotte Convention said, "The issue of suffrage is not altogether one of polling. It is one of right."

Gov. Samuel T. Crawford said, "There is no reason in law or ethics which should exclude Negroes from all the rights that others enjoy who are no more worthy because of their race or color."

Samuel Wood organized the Impartial Suffrage Association in Topeka in 1867 for equal voting rights "without regard to sex, race or color." Despite his efforts the 1867 electorate rejected his amendment to remove the racial qualifications for voting. It was favored by only seven of the 44 counties. Shawnee was not one of the seven.

In 1869 Gov. James M. Harvey proclaimed before the Legislature that "there should be no monopoly of political power in our own favored class of white male citizens." However the word "white" remained affixed to the suffrage law in Kansas until 1888, which was 18 years after the Constitution of the United States declared black people voters. Another governor, Thomas A. Osborn, called discrimination "a relic of barbarism."

In 1865 Negro and white children went to the same school, a two-story building on Sixth between Kansas and Quincy. In 1866 the black children were moved to the top floor, which was the beginning of segregation. Topeka had segregated schools before the Legislature gave school boards the authority to maintain them.

Sen. Jacob Winter called his fellow senators the favored segregation scum and dregs of slavery deeply seated in their unregenerative natures." He censored all discrimination, thought it "unconscionable that citizens of intelligence, culture and moral worth are rejected from hotel tables and places of amusement and treated with indignity for no reason other than that the creator gave them a different color from ours."

—October 12, 1982

*   *   *

Last Sunday I had an important telephone call from my grandson Jim in Florida about the physical condition of a member of the family.

I'll say this for Jim. He didn't hem and haw, didn't ask if it was cold enough up here, didn't inquire about my cat Fancy (and he loves cats), nor did he seem interested in anything that might be going on in Topeka.

He just came right out, manly and straightforward, and in a clear calm voice said what he had to say:

"Adrianne has her first tooth."

A few moments later he added, quietly and in even voice, "Barbara gave her a drink of water and heard the tooth clink against the glass." Adrianne is his daughter. She was five months old Jan. 9.

—January 20, 1983

Pockets

A notable invention was the pocket. Could it have come from observing the pouch of the kangaroo? A man's suit with vest has 15 pockets — how useful to have that safe watch pocket and the little pocket inside another pocket for tickets. A woman's suit has two pockets, sometimes four, her dresses two, but more often none at all.

Honesty forces me to pause and ask what man's useful adaptation of the pocket and woman's small use of it says. Instead of utilizing the great convenience, women chose the handbag. It has to be carried, is always in the way, contents jumbled together, always being lost or snatched. Man left his hands free, to fight if necessary or to carry the packages she cannot manage because she has to carry that big handbag.

Do you suppose that right there may have been the beginning of what we now are calling discrimination? Do you suppose that man, showing himself more imaginative, more adaptive, may have started to plunge ahead and take the reins? Could our failure to make maximum use of the pocket be why we need the ratification of three more states?

This is too painful a topic. I shall not dwell on it.

—February 9, 1983

Fancy

One of life's minor pleasures is a cat sleeping on your lap. If it is your own cat, it marks the measure of confidence between you. If it is a strange cat, you feel honored by his trust.

When Fancy comes and stands by the chair with an upward look I know that she is about to leap into my lap. She makes herself comfortable and immediately goes to sleep. Sleep comes instantly to a cat. If Fancy is lying in another chair when I sit down, she waits about a minute, then comes to my lap.

She has soft thick fur done in a tasteful arrangement of dark gray and white, with an inverted white V on her face. A touch of smudge around her eyes hints of mascara. She curls up to sleep, her head tucked down, her tail outlining the circle.

The physical warmth of her sleeping on my lap is pleasant and comforting and she does not wake as I touch or smooth her fur. At any loud noise she is instantly alert and springs down to be ready for flight or combat. If it is a more moderate noise, she raises her head and, seeing no cause for anxiety, goes back to sleep.

She likes to sit on a table by a window and look out. What does she see out there, hour after hour, day after day? What does she think of the outdoors? How does it look to her? What does she see in me? A convenience, a source of food, someone to open doors and provide a lap to sit on?

—March 14, 1983

* * *

My great-grandson, Matt Stevens, age 4, had a sad complaint. He was saying, "Everybody but me has got money." His sister April, 6, had a dollar bill and a few coins. His parents and grandparents were going out and bringing things home, a sign of having money. But he had none.

"Just wait," April consoled him. "Pretty soon your teeth will start falling out; then you'll have money."

—July 7, 1983

Fifty Years

Back in September John Stauffer said to me, "Save October 31. That's the date of your first column and we're going to do some celebrating."

That day is here, marking fifty years of writing a column six days a week. People have asked if that is a record. One said, "You claim it and see if anybody disputes you."

Writing a column these fifty years has been like a bright kaleidoscope of life, with warm and friendly exchanges with readers. They write letters, they talk to me. I hear about joys and sorrows and about the cute thing their grandchild said. They tell me to go outside and see that bright star just above the moon. Some want me to take up their cudgels, "but don't mention my name." A shy little girl said, "I've never had my name in the paper." She had it there a few days later.

Readers have given me seeds, flowers and plants, food fresh from their gardens, food cooked and portions of meat from almost every edible animal and some that my husband questioned as edible. They have given me handkerchiefs and scarves, books, pictures and nice old embroidery. And they have brought boxes and boxes of their old clippings, saying "I know you like things like these."

I understand they can't bear to drown their own kittens, so I take them and store them in the sunroom.

Column writing can be risky. There is danger of falling into a rut. If a few readers have spoken well of your columns on morals, you may get the notion that you hold the bottle of liniment that will ease the troubles of the world and begin dosing it out in your best pulpit manner. Or you can slide into that slick grove of cliches and put out old jokes that bored Abraham.

Anyway, dear readers, here we are at this happy occasion. The Capital-Journal is hosting a reception at the Ramada Inn from four to six this afternoon. I couldn't have got here without you and I hope you will come and share the pleasure with me. I think they have whipped up an extra cake.

—October 31, 1983